# Higher and Higher

Skills and Practice for the
OXFORD HIGHER CERTIFICATE
and
ARELS HIGHER CERTIFICATE
examinations

Roy Kingsbury and Guy Wellman

# Students' Book

D1666595

Longman

**Longman Group UK Ltd**
*Longman House, Burnt Mill, Harlow,*
*Essex CM20 2JE, England*
*and Associated Companies throughout*
*the world*

First published 1990

ISBN 0 582 05485 0


*Set in 10/13 New Century Schoolbook (Postscript) Linotype*

*Produced by Longman Singapore Publishers (Pte) Ltd.*
*Printed in Singapore*

## Acknowledgements

We are grateful to the folllowing for permission to reproduce copyright material:
British Telecom plc for 'Important Notice' distributed to British Telecom Solent; Channel 4 TV for extract from the article 'Command and Control of Nuclear Weapons' in *Equinox* booklet 1987; Consumers' Association for extracts from 'Take the Credit' pages 248-9 *Which?*, May 1987 & 'FLorida' pages 6-7 *Holiday Which?* January 1990; Express Newspapers plc for extracts from articles 'Food for Life' in *Sunday Express Magazine* 19.2.89 & '2010 This is the face' page 7 *Sunday Express* 17.7.88; Headway Publications Ltd for an extract from the article 'Peak Enjoyment' page 43 NatWest *Moneycare* magazine © Headway Publications Ltd; J. Sainsbury plc for an extract from the article 'Facts about Food Additives' in Sainsbury's *Living Today* No. 6; Independent Television Publications Ltd for an edited extract from 'Films' column by David Quinlan page 6 *TV Times* 17.12.88-1.1.89; Listings Ltd for an extract from 'Arts and Entertainment Guide' in *The Guardian* 17.1.89 © Listings Ltd; Longman Group UK Ltd for two definitions from *Longman Dictionary of Contemporary English* 1978; Newspaper Publishing plc for extract from the article 'No place like home for going to school' by Simon Midgley in *The Independent* 12.11.87; Times Newspapers Ltd for article 'The Cottage Chatelaine' by Brian Collett in *The Times* 9.10.87, extract from 'Advice by Phone' (Booklet page 15), article 'Will a Sunnier Britain Warm to the Cafe Culture?' by Amit Roy *The Sunday Times* 13.11.88, adapted extracts from the articles 'GCSE triumph for dyslexic teenager' by David Tytler *The Times* 30.8.88, 'Britain's teachers are as thick as the rest of us' by Tim Rayment *The Sunday Times* 13.10.88, 'Tune in for your trial' by Matthew May *The Times* 30.8.88, 'Home is where the work is' by Caroline McGhie *The Sunday Times* 18.9.88, 'Young Britain' by Greg Hadfield & Tim Rayment *The Sunday Times* 13.11.88 & 'Too fast, too soon' by Edward Fennell *The Times* 17.11.88 all © Times Newspapers Ltd 1987, 1988.
We are grateful to the following, for permission to reproduce copyright photographs:
"Reproduced with kind permission of Benckiser Limited", for page 75. Bristol Evening Post for page 27. Colorific/Olag Soot – Black Star, for page 11 (main), and /Marcus Brooke for page 11 (inset). Collins Publishers/SAS Survival Handbook by John Wiseman for page 77. Columbia Pictures Industries Inc for page 68. The Consumer Association for pages 65 and 93. Greg Evans Photo Library for page 92. The Ronald Grant Archive for pages 23 and 89. "Courtesy of the Natural History Museum, London for page 24. "Reproduced with kind permission of The Radio Times', for page 58. © Times Newspapers Limited 1987/The Times 9.10.87 – Mike Charity for page 53, and /The Times 6.11.87 for page 76. © Times Newspapers Limited 1988/The Times 30.8.88 – Peter Trievnor for page 35, and/The Sunday Times 13.11.88 for pages 60-61. © Times Newspapers Limited 1989/The Times 3.7.89 for page 71. "Copyright 1988 USA Today, reprinted with permission", for page 81. "Reproduced with the kind permission of Zanussi Limited for page 75 (inset).

# Contents

# Introduction for Students

## WHO IS THIS BOOK FOR?

*Higher and Higher* is written for Advanced students of English who are intending to take the Oxford Higher Certificate examination, the ARELS Higher Certificate examination, or both. This means that, as they are both higher level exams, you will probably have taken (or at least reached the level of) the Cambridge First Certificate before you begin to prepare for either of them.

In addition, the book provides valuable practice for any post-FCE students or those of you going on to take other Advanced level examinations.

## WHAT IS THE AIM OF THE BOOK?

The book is *not* a set of practice tests or exams. Its aim is to provide you with guidance and essential practice in the skills that you will have to employ in the two examinations.

If you are planning to take only one of the exams, you will still find that both Oxford and ARELS sections of Units will be useful for you. The (Oxford) reading and writing activities complement the (ARELS) listening and speaking activities, and vice versa.

## WHAT DOES EACH EXAM CONSIST OF?

Your teacher will explain in detail what each exam involves, but here is a brief outline:

The **Oxford Higher Examination** tests reading and writing. The exam has two Papers: **Paper One** tests mainly writing, often in response to one or more reading texts; and **Paper Two** concentrates on tests of reading, very often with a 'dictionary question' to see how well you can use an English-English dictionary.

The **ARELS Higher Certificate** is a test of listening and speaking which lasts about an hour. The exam is divided into six sections which include giving a short talk on a topic, responding to situations, listening comprehension, reading aloud and telling a story from pictures.

## HOW IS THE BOOK ORGANISED AND HOW DOES IT PREPARE YOU FOR THE EXAMS?

There are twelve Units in the book (see Contents page). Each Unit consists of 6 pages: 4 pages in each are devoted to Oxford preparation, 2 pages to ARELS preparation. However, although each begins with a 'Warm-up' session, the shape of each Unit is not always the same. Some Units begin with speaking and listening (ARELS exam preparation) while alternate Units begin with reading and writing (Oxford exam preparation).

SPECIAL NOTE: All 'O' sections in a Unit (O1, O2, etc.) are activities and exercises primarily connected with the Oxford Higher exam: all 'A' sections (A1, A2, etc.) are primarily connected with the ARELS Higher exam.

At the end of the book there are two complete Practice Exams (an Oxford and an ARELS) for use just before you take the exam itself.

You are allowed to use a dictionary in the Oxford exam, so there is a section called 'Using an English-English dictionary' at the beginning of the book, and most Units contain a 'dictionary work' phase.

If you study the table opposite, you will see that, instead of concentrating on any one aspect of either of the exams in just one Unit, we have spread guidance and practice throughout the book.

## WHAT WILL YOU BE EXPECTED TO DO IN CLASS?

A lot of the activities in the course will involve your working with a partner or working in a group. Sharing ideas with other students is very important at this level, and you should find you benefit a great deal from working with fellow students.

A **Tapescript** is provided at the end of the book for reference after you have done the exercises in class.

**Answers to exercises** in all Units are given in the **Key** in the Teacher's Handbook.

| OXFORD HIGHER CERTIFICATE | Preparation in *Higher and Higher* Units (and pages) |
|---|---|
| **Dictionary work** | **1** (8 & 10); **2** (14); **3** (20 & 22); **4** (26); **6** (41); **8** (50-51); **9** (56); **10** (62); **12** (78) |

## PAPER 1*

| | |
|---|---|
| **1** Write a report, letter, article, etc. with little or no input/reading matter | **3** (22-23); **11** (72) |
| **2** Write letters and notes (formal and informal) based on reading matter | **2** (14-17); **3** (24); **4** (28); **5** (36); **8** (50-51); **9** (58-59); **12** (77) |
| **3** Various kinds of notes and messages to colleagues and friends, ads., etc. | **2** (15); **3** (25); **5** (34); **7** (46); **10** (64) |

## PAPER 2*

| | |
|---|---|
| **1** Read a report, for example, and extract information to write letters | **1** (12-13); **4** (27-28); **6** (39); **7** (47-49); **8** (52-53); **12** (75-77) |
| **2** Read a text (e.g. a leaflet) and answer questions in different forms | **1** (10-11); **2** (16-17); **3** (24-25); **4** (26-27); **5** (35); **7** (46); **8** (52-53); **9** (59-61); **10** (64-65); **11** (70-71) |
| **3** Fill in the blanks in a text | **1** (10-11); **6** (40-41); **10** (62-63); **11** (73) |
| **4** Read a text and write the questions | **8** (52-53) |
| **5** Vocabulary exercises/tests | **3** (25); **5** (36-37); **9** (59-61) |
| **6** Read a text and correct errors | **8** (50-51) |
| **7** Matching exercises | **5** (36-37); **6** (38-41); **10** (64-65); **11** (70-71); **12** (74-75) |

| ARELS HIGHER CERTIFICATE | Preparation in *Higher and Higher* Units (and pages) |
|---|---|

## Section

| | |
|---|---|
| **1** Giving a short persuasive talk | **4** (30-31); **8** (55); **12** (79) |
| **2** Part 1: Responding to remarks<br>Part 2: Responding to situations<br>Part 3: Taking part in a conversation | **1** (8); **6** (42); **9** (57)<br>**1** (9); **5** (32); **9** (57)<br>**8** (54-55); **10** (66) |
| **3** Reading aloud part of a dialogue | **2** (18-19); **7** (44-45); **10** (67) |
| **4** Listening to an interview<br>Other listening tests | **5** (33); **9** (56); **12** (78)<br>**4** (31); **5** (33); **7** (44-45); **12** (78) |
| **5** Telling a story from pictures | **3** (20-21); **6** (42-43); **11** (68-69) |
| **6** 'Oral grammar' exercises | **3** (21); **6** (43); **8** (55); **11** (68-69); **12** (79) |

---

\* The numbers under the Oxford Papers 1 and 2 do not refer to sections, but to typical kinds of test exercise that occur in those Papers.

# Using an English-English Dictionary

*words and phrases in poetry which are not used in special PROSE or speech*
**dic·tion·a·ry** /ˈdɪkʃənəri‖-neri/ *n* **1** a book that gives a list of words in alphabetical order, with their pronunciations and meanings: *This book is a dictionary* **2** a book like this that gives, for each word, one in another language with the same *meaning...* a book

*INTRODUCTION*

**1  Answer these questions, then discuss them in pairs and with the class:**

1  Did you use an English-English dictionary when you first started to learn the language? Why?/Why not?
2  When did you start using an English-English dictionary?
3  Why is an English-English dictionary particularly important for Advanced students, do you think?
4  When do you think native speakers of English use a dictionary? (When do *you* use a dictionary in your own language?)

**2  Read this paragraph and compare your answers (above) with the opinions in it:**

Being able to use an English-English dictionary is a very important skill, especially for Advanced students of the language. It doesn't matter whether you are taking an examination or not: you will still read and hear lots of words in English that you don't understand and that you will need or want to look up. And when you're writing something in English, you may want to look for a word or you may want to check the spelling. (Many native English speakers often use a dictionary to check spellings.) You might want to find out the construction that follows a particular word, how it's pronounced or whether it can be a verb as well as a noun or an adjective. So, if you are going to enter an examination like the Oxford Higher, then it is vital that you learn to use an English-English dictionary with ease and confidence.

Why is it vital for you to learn to use an English-English dictionary if you are going to take the Oxford Higher exam?

*SOME PROBLEMS AND TASKS*

**The following short exercises will help you to familiarise yourself with your English-English dictionary and remind you of the many things it can do.**

**1  Check the basic meaning of a word**
You may meet a word or two in a sentence which you do not recognise at all.

> Don't be tempted to conceal anything because goods which aren't properly declared may be confiscated by Customs.

You might first guess the meaning of *conceal* and *confiscate*.
What do you think *conceal* means: show? steal? hide? report? disguise?
What do you think *confiscate* means: burn? steal? destroy? report? take away?

**Check the meanings in your English-English dictionary to see if you were right.**

## 2 Check parts of speech

When you see the words in the chart, which part of speech do you think of first: verb? noun? adjective? adverb?

**Use your dictionary to check or find out how many ways these words can be used, and complete the chart.**

|  | n. | v. | adj. | adv. |
|---|---|---|---|---|
| rebel | ✔ | ✔ | ✔ | — |
| well |  |  |  |  |
| contract |  |  |  |  |
| milk |  |  |  |  |
| long |  |  |  |  |
| hare |  |  |  |  |
| frequent |  |  |  |  |

## 3 Check the precise meaning of words

**Look at this incomplete sentence:**

*The freshly fallen snow was .......... in the early morning sunlight.*

**In your head there are probably several 'shining' words. Use your dictionary to help you choose the best one from these:**

*glaring   glowing   glistening   flashing   twinkling   flickering*

## 4 Check collocation

**Certain words often go with others comfortably (we say they collocate), but uncomfortably, if at all, with others. With the help of your dictionary decide which of these nouns go well after the adjective *blunt*.**

*pencil   pain   surface   person   question   joke   remark   praise   knife*

## 5 Check pronunciation

**Your dictionary will show you how a word is pronounced, probably just after the head-word. Do any of these words rhyme? Use your dictionary to find out.**

*bough   hiccough   trough   rough   thorough   dough*

## 6 Check the construction that follows a word

**A dictionary can help you use a word correctly in English. Use your dictionary to check which of these sentences is/are acceptable with the word *intention*.**

**a** I had an intention to speak to him.   **c** I have no intention of spending my life here.

**b** It wasn't my intention to upset you.   **d** My intention is not upsetting him.

## 7 Check spelling

The two words underlined in this sentence look (and are!) wrong.
**Use your dictionary to check or find out the correct spellings.**

The <u>accomadation</u> was very poor and bore no <u>ressemblence</u> to the description in your brochure.

**Now do the same with the words in the box: they are all spelt wrongly.**

> *heigth*
> *incredable*
> *precausions*
> *disasterous*
> *alkaholic*

# UNIT 1 Sports and Leisure

### WARM-UP

**As a class, in small groups or in pairs, make a list of as many sports as you can and list what we call the people who take part in them. Then briefly discuss one or two of these questions:**

- Is there a 'national sport' in your country? If so, what is it? Do many people take part in it, or is it mainly a 'spectator sport'?
- What sports do you (or did you) have to take part in at school? Do/Did you enjoy doing sport? Why?/Why not?
- Which sports do you enjoy a) taking part in? and b) watching?
- What do you understand by the words 'amateur' and 'professional' when applied to sportsmen and women?

*A1*   **Look at the ways in which we use *So ...* and *Neither/Nor ...* to agree with other people's opinions, likes, dislikes and so on.**

| | |
|---|---|
| I can swim quite well.<br>So can I. | I can't play tennis.<br>Neither/Nor can I. |
| I like watching ice hockey.<br>So do I. | I don't watch football very often.<br>Neither/Nor do I. |

*A2*   **Listen to the cassette and notice carefully how the woman agrees with the man. How are the words *am, have, had, can* and *was* pronounced in *So am I*, etc.?**

*A3*   **Agree with these statements in the same way, using *So ...* or *Neither/Nor ...* :**

1 I like watching tennis.
2 I just don't understand cricket.
3 I must try and get into the team.
4 I'm useless at sports.
5 I've never played lawn tennis.

6 I can't play hockey at all.
7 I haven't tried water skiing yet.
8 I'd like to try scuba diving.
9 I should do more exercise.
10 I didn't watch the Olympics on TV.

*A4*   **Now listen to the cassette and agree with what other people say about sport.**

A5  Below (in A6) are some sports-related situations in which you might find yourself. Since you will need to make a suggestion, an invitation, etc., study first some of the ways in which you can do these things:

| **Suggesting** | I suggest we have<br>Might I suggest we have<br>Let's have<br>Why don't we have | } a game of tennis tomorrow(?) |
| **Inviting** | Would you like to come<br>How about/What about coming<br>Do you fancy coming | } to the match tomorrow? |
| **Accepting/<br>Refusing an<br>invitation** | Yes, I would/Yes, I'd love to. Thank you very much.<br>No, I'm sorry, I can't [this afternoon], I'm afraid. [I have to stay home and do some tidying up.] | |

Which of the sentences or questions above would you use to a friend and which to a stranger, acquaintance or someone in authority? Try to explain why.

Now think of two or three different ways that you could

a) apologise to someone;
b) congratulate someone;
c) commiserate or sympathise with someone;
d) give someone advice.

Again, which would you use to a friend, and which to an acquaintance or stranger?

A6  You're studying at an English language school. What would you say in the situations below? Read each and decide a) what you have to do - apologise? make a suggestion? offer advice? etc., and b) whether the situation is formal or informal. Then suggest different ways to respond appropriately.

1  You have booked a squash court to play with a friend this evening, but he/she has let you down, so you ask another friend. What do you say to him/her?
2  You're supposed to be playing in the school football team tomorrow afternoon, but have just sprained your ankle badly. What do you say when you ring up the sports teacher?
3  A good friend of yours has just been advised by a doctor to take up a sport in order to lose weight. You do a lot of sport, so he or she asks your advice about what to take up. What do you say?
4  A friend knows you enjoy watching the local ice hockey team and has just invited you to the game this evening. What do you say?
5  You've agreed to be the referee or umpire for an inter-school table tennis or billiards competition. You have been distracted and are not sure what the score is in a match. What do you say when the players ask you the score?

A7  Now listen to the cassette and respond to some more similar situations.

*01*   **Dictionary work**

1  **When you are reading English, there will be words that you think you understand (or you can guess what they mean), and there will be other words that you will never have met before and that you will not understand. Use your English-English dictionary to check on or find out the meanings of these words:**

a) a charge card/a credit card  b) a venue  c) to muster  d) frenetic  e) a fell  f) to extrude  g) a cobbler  h) crampons  i) gaiters

2  **Some of the following words are spelt correctly, others are spelt incorrectly. Which are which? First, sort them into nouns, verbs, adjectives and adverbs. Some may appear in more than one group. Then use your dictionary to check the spellings.**

a) exsciting  b) canoing  c) professional  d) supervition  e) suitible  f) reasonably  g) caveing  h) dissregard  i) absence  j) identefy

*02*   **Opposite is the first page of a magazine article written in October 1988. Read the whole page first to get the gist of it, then do the exercises below.**
**Remember that you may use your English-English dictionary if you wish, but always make an effort to work out the meanings of unknown words from the context first.**

1  There is a double meaning in the title of the article *'Peak Enjoyment'*. Can you explain it?

2  Read paragraphs 1 and 2 and find a suitable word or short phrase for each blank. There may be a variety of possible completions, so discuss your answers with a partner and then with the class.

3  Read the rest of the article and answer these questions. Discuss your answers, which should be as brief as possible, with a partner and the class.

a)  How new is mountaineering as a sport?
b)  What proof does the writer give that 'the uplands of Britain have never been so popular'?
c)  What attracts people to the hills?
d)  Why was equipment cheap when the writer started hill walking?
e)  How is the situation different nowadays?
f)  How much would you expect to pay now for a pair of walking boots?
g)  When must a walker or climber wear boots with rigid or semi-rigid soles?
h)  Explain in your own words the phrase 'will set you back up to £150'.
i)  What are 'gaiters' and why are they often necessary?
j)  You only have the first page of the article. What do you think the rest of it will be about? Why?

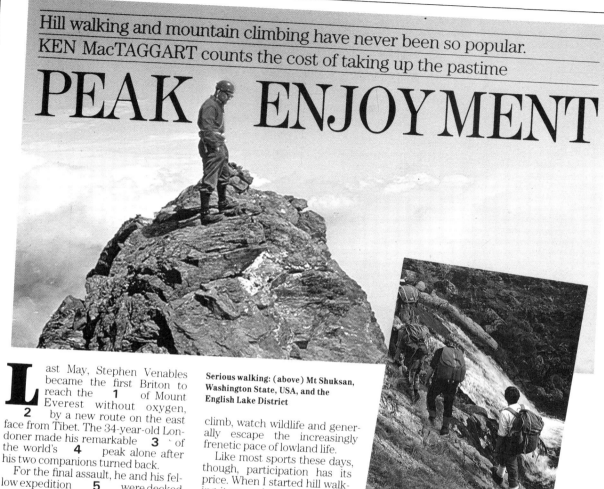

## Hill walking and mountain climbing have never been so popular. KEN MacTAGGART counts the cost of taking up the pastime

# PEAK ENJOYMENT

**Serious walking: (above) Mt Shuksan, Washington State, USA, and the English Lake District**

**L**ast May, Stephen Venables became the first Briton to reach the **1** of Mount Everest without oxygen, **2** by a new route on the east face from Tibet. The 34-year-old Londoner made his remarkable **3** of the world's **4** peak alone after his two companions turned back.

For the final assault, he and his fellow expedition **5** were decked out in about £2,000-worth of clothes and **6**, which **7** Rolex watches and a charge card. Venables wore five **8** of specialist clothing, much of which is commercially **9**

**10** to the increasing numbers of and climbers who take to the hills for enjoyment.

It took the human race a long time to shake off its natural fear of high places. Though the Olympics started 3,000 years ago, mountaineering as a sport is barely 200 years old in the Alps, and dates back just a century in Britain. Nowadays, the uplands of Britain have never been so popular as a venue for recreation. The Ramblers' Association and the British Mountaineering Council can muster 100,000 members between them, but the true number of participants is anything up to ten times that number. They take to the hills regularly to walk,

climb, watch wildlife and generally escape the increasingly frenetic pace of lowland life.

Like most sports these days, though, participation has its price. When I started hill walking, it was a cheap day out. All it took was the bus fare to a range of nearby hills and the most basic of gear, largely culled from army surplus stores – a second-hand combat jacket which had seen service in the Vietnam War, a crudely-stitched pair of crippling commando boots, ex-police trousers with sponge-like properties of moisture retention, a leather motorbike helmet and a plastic mac.

That would not do for present day walkers and climbers, who each weekend invade the moors and fells dressed in the latest gaily-coloured designer anoraks and breeches. Their underwear has been developed in a laboratory and their boots have been extruded on a production line under the eye of a plastics technician, with a cobbler nowhere in sight.

Cheap leather boots start at around £20, but a serious fell walker will probably want something more durable

like the Zamberlan Fell Lite, which comes with a Vibram moulded rubber sole, at about £60. However, these are inadequate for winter climbing and a rigid or semi-rigid sole is necessary to take crampons. Modern plastic boots such as Koflach or the Scarpa Grinta Extrem, which has a removable inner boot, will set you back up to £150.

Gaiters are a useful adjunct to boots – helpful when walking through vegetation and for keeping snow out in winter, and with the best you can even ford streams dryshod. They vary from £12 to £50.

Body coverings have been revolutionised over the past decade by an entirely new concept in clothing. The high-tech walker wears synthetic fibre underwear which acts like a wick to draw off the chilling moisture from perspiration. An artificial pile jacket ▶

O3 **A week ago Pat returned from an activity holiday. Read the information below, then write the two letters O4 and O5.**

**1** This is part of the brochure for the holiday:

# Folly Farm Activity Holidays

Over the years, thousands of young people from all over the world have enjoyed our fun-packed, exciting activity holidays. 'Folly Farm' is situated on the banks of Lake Folly and close to the Hazard Hills, a popular area for ramblers, riders and climbers. We have all kinds of sports and sporting activities to choose from: tennis, climbing, walking, canoeing, riding, caving, sailing, wind-surfing, water-skiing – all with professional coaching and supervision, and all equipment supplied. Suitable for the 13-19 age group.

**2** This is part of the questionnaire that Pat completed:

5 How satisfied were you with your holiday as a whole?
Not at all satisfied __ Reasonably satisifed ✔ Very satisfied __
6 How would you rate the range of sports and activities offered?
Very poor __ Poor __ Good ✔ Very good __ Excellent __
7 How would you rate the standard of accommodation and food?
Very poor __ Poor ✔ Good __ Very good __ Excellent __
8 Which of the following did you take part in?
tennis __ climbing ✔ canoeing ✔ riding ✔ caving __
sailing __ windsurfing __ water-skiing __ walking __
9 How would you describe the standard of coaching and tuition offered?
Very poor __ Poor ✔ Good __ Very good __ Excellent __
10 Would you come to 'Folly Farm' again? Yes __ No ✔
If you have ticked 'No', please write your comments overpage – and be honest! How else can we improve our service in the future?

**3** This is part of an accident report filed by the leader of Pat's group:

While the majority of the youngsters were very well-behaved and followed my instructions to the letter, I have to report that a small group of four, of which Pat was one, tended to disregard my advice on safety and the need to stay with the main party. This was the first time that many of the party had ever been climbing, Pat included, so the route I chose to the summit was relatively easy. Nevertheless, as I warned them, there were places where the rocks were unsafe, which is why we should keep together. Before I could stop them, Pat and her friends decided to go their own way at one point. I had just noticed their absence when I heard a scream from below me. I rushed back and found that Pat had slipped off the path and was lying on a small ledge. I managed to climb down quite easily. Pat was frightened, but not badly injured.

*O4*　**Imagine you are Pat. Since sending off the questionnaire, you have revised some of your opinions. In fact you might now consider going on one of their holidays again and would certainly recommend them. Using the information opposite, write a letter (about 200 words) to the holiday organisers.**
**Before you begin, discuss these questions with a partner, and make notes:**

1  Is the letter going to be formal or informal?
2  Where do you write your address?
3  Who are you going to write to? Where do they live? (Is their address necessary for your letter? Why/Why not? If an address is necessary, make one up.)
4  How will you write the date, and where will you put it?
5  How will you address the person you are writing to? And how will you end the letter?
6  Now about the content: here are some points you might put into the letter. Where should they go - at the beginning (para. 1), in the middle (para. 2, or 2 and 3), or at the end (para. 3, or 4)? Re-order the points and suggest some of the language you might use:

■ Correct the impression you gave in the questionnaire.
■ Ask for their brochure for next year.
■ Thank the 'Folly Farm' staff for a good holiday.
■ Apologise for causing trouble while climbing.
■ Tell them you'll recommend 'Folly Farm' to your friends.
■ Say why you are writing.
■ Compare the sports/activities at 'Folly Farm' with those at school.

**Now work with a partner to write the letter. Both contribute language, discuss, correct each other, etc.**

*O5*　**Still imagine that you are Pat. Write a letter (of about 200 words) to a close friend in a fairly light-hearted manner telling him or her about the holiday and in particular about your accident.**
**Before you begin, discuss these questions with a partner:**

1  Is the letter going to be formal or informal?
2  Who are you going to write to? Where does he or she live? (Is his/her address necessary for your letter? Why/Why not?)
3  Where will you put the date and how will you write it?
4  How will you address the person you are writing to? How will you end the letter?
5  Now answer these questions and make notes in order to write a rough draft:
　　a) Why are you writing to your friend?
　　b) What was the holiday like (in general)?
　　c) When did you go? How long did you stay? When did you come back?
　　d) What did you do there?
　　e) Did you have any strange, funny or frightening experiences while you were there? Briefly describe one.
　　f) Would you recommend the holiday/place to your friend? Are you going to invite him or her to go with you next year?

**Now write the letter.**

# UNIT 2  Money Matters

### WARM-UP

**As a class, in small groups or in pairs, do some of these exercises:**

1 What can you 'do' with money? Think of as many verbs as you can to replace 'spend' in this sentence: 'You can *spend* it.'

2 How many currencies can you think of? Add to these: Great Britain/the UK – £ (pound) sterling; the USA – US$ (dollar); ...

3 How many ways can you buy things? Add to this: You can pay cash; ....

4 If you were lucky enough to win some money, but one condition was that you *had to* save it, how could you invest it? List some possibilities.

5 See how many words you can add to the two lists on the right before comparing your lists with a partner's. The two lists are possible sources of income and outgoings in a three-generation household.

INCOME
Husband's salary
Grandmother's pension
Dividends on shares

OUTGOINGS
Income tax
Mortgage
Insurance premiums

O1  **Dictionary work**

1 **The notice opposite was sent to telephone users in the South of England. Read it and use your English-English dictionary to check on or find out the meanings of any words you do not understand.**

2 **The following words are all to do with money. Some are spelt correctly, others incorrectly. Which are which? Use your dictionary to check the spellings.**

a) (bank) overdraught  b) current account  c) credite card  d) repayment
e) borrow  f) finanse company

3 **Some dictionaries list all abbreviations in an Appendix or a special section at the end. In others (e.g. the *Longman Dictionary of Contemporary English*), you will find them mixed in alphabetically with all other words. Use your dictionary to find out what these mean and how they are pronounced:**

a/c;  10 c;  20° C;  e.g.;  10 ft;  100 Fr;  IOU;
3 m;  M6;  5 mm;  mpg;  mph;  EEC;  Ltd;

O2  **Read the notice opposite again. You are sharing a flat with three other students.**

1 Write to British Telecom, Solent, for further clarification of the new system. You are concerned about payment as you are all on a tight budget.

2 Now write an arresting (but polite) note (not more than 20 words) to stick on the wall by the phone reminding all users of the cost of phone-calls.

**IMPORTANT NOTICE**

**Dear Customer**
**We are introducing a major new computer system which will enable us to handle your enquiries more efficiently and responsively. During the introduction of this system our bill production schedule will be disrupted. To cater for this you may notice that your next bill will be produced a little earlier. Whilst the rental charging date will be unchanged the call charges may be lower than expected because your meter will have been read earlier than usual. There will naturally be a catching up exercise in future telephone bills after the system has been installed.**

**This may affect your budgeting for our bill payments and we apologise for any inconvenience this may cause you.**

**BRITISH TELECOM**
**SOLENT**

O3    **Note the kinds of word we can omit when we are writing a short, informal note. Then convert the sentences that follow into note form.**

I haven't forgotten that I owe you five pounds. My parents are sending me some money and I'll pay you back when the cheque arrives.

> I.O.U. £5. Haven't forgotten.
> Parents sending money.
> Will pay you back when
> cheque arrives.

1  I received Mr Jones' offer today. It isn't a bad one. I think we should go ahead.
2  The tickets for the show cost £5. I've bought two. You can pay me when it's convenient.
3  We need your help, because our gas bill is astronomical. Is there any chance of a loan?
4  The garage want us to settle their bill, so I've left the cheque book on the shelf by the refrigerator. I'll see you at eight o'clock at the supermarket entrance. I think we'll have to pay for this week's shopping by credit card.

04   This questionnaire was conducted by a popular daily newspaper on attitudes to spending money. Read it and answer yes or no for each question. Then count up the total number of yeses and noes that you scored.

£$£$   **How careful are you with your money?**   £$£$

|  | | Yes | No |
|---|---|---|---|
| **Do you** | | | |
| 1 | buy in bulk whenever possible to beat inflation? | ☐ | ☐ |
| 2 | collect packet tops that offer a discount on your next purchase? | ☐ | ☐ |
| 3 | look out for special offers, '5p off' labels, gift vouchers, etc.? | ☐ | ☐ |
| 4 | buy economy-size products that are a few p. cheaper per kilo or litre? | ☐ | ☐ |
| 5 | look out for credit deals that have especially favourable interest rates? | ☐ | ☐ |
| 6 | fill your tank before an anticipated petrol price rise? | ☐ | ☐ |
| 7 | shop only where money can be refunded rather than goods exchanged? | ☐ | ☐ |
| 8 | delay payment of bills until the final demand? | ☐ | ☐ |
| 9 | take holidays out of season — at a fraction of the normal cost? | ☐ | ☐ |
| 10 | change foreign currency when the exchange rate is most favourable? | ☐ | ☐ |
| 11 | consult your bank statement regularly to make sure all is well? | ☐ | ☐ |
| 12 | look out for bargains and genuine reductions in seasonal sales? | ☐ | ☐ |
| 13 | phone at cheap-rate times, reversing the charges when you can? | ☐ | ☐ |

05   **Here is an extract from the newspaper's commentary on people's scores.**
**Write suitable comments for the two missing score bands.**

over 12  yeses :   You *are* careful with your money, aren't you?! You still believe you can get something for nothing these days.

9 – 12 :   ..................................................................................................................

5 – 8 :   ..................................................................................................................

under 5 :   You must be a millionaire, or have more money than sense!

06   **Collate the results of at least six other students. Write an article summarising your findings and drawing conclusions. Try using phrases like these:**

| | | |
|---|---|---|
| a large majority | (not) surprisingly | the results suggest that ... |
| nearly four out of five | naturally enough | according to our findings ... |
| some two-thirds | broadly speaking | it would appear that ... |
| only one in three | on the whole | our survey found that ... |

07   **Taking your information from the text opposite, answer these questions:**

1 Which lending system seems to offer the largest loans?
2 What's one disadvantage of a bank overdraft?
3 Explain 'authorised' when applied to a bank overdraft.
4 Which form of borrowing might please the bank least and embarrass you most?
5 Businesses may get tax relief on credit card loan interest. True or false?
6 Arrangement fees would add to the cost of the loan. True or false?
7 Which lending method has the highest APR? Why is this so?
8 Which lending scheme has the lowest APR? What is the main drawback with this scheme?

## Loans and lenders in detail

**BEST BUY BORROWING**

**Bank ordinary loan** – the money is paid into your current account; you make regular, fixed repayments into a separate loan account. A good form of flexible, longer-term borrowing – but not always available.
APR 15 to 20% (variable).
Arranged individually, so you may be able to negotiate it to suit your needs exactly; you may be able to borrow more than with other types of loan and for as long as 10 years
BUT banks tend not to advertise these; they may try to persuade you to get a personal loan instead; they may require security; you might have to pay arrangement fees.

**Bank overdraft** – going into the red on your current account. See *Bank charges Update*, p258. Convenient, but can work out expensive in the long-term.
APR 17 to 25% (variable) if authorised by manager; may be more if unauthorised. Bank charges will put the cost up even more.

Quick to arrange; can be fairly cheap if authorised; security not usually needed; available for any purpose
BUT you'll have to pay bank charges; there's no tax relief on interest unless loan is for business purpose; possible arrangement fee; bank can insist you pay it off at any time.

**Credit cards** – eg Visa, Access – see *Which?* September 1985 p390.
APR 26.8% on unpaid balances; 26.8% on cash advances (Access), 27.2% (Visa). Interest rate is variable.
Quick and convenient; can give interest-free credit for up to eight weeks; no arrangement fees; no set repayment schedule; cash advances and personal loans may be available; no security required
BUT you can't use them everywhere; there's no tax relief on interest unless loan is for a business purpose; can get expensive if you don't regularly pay off what you owe.

**Charge cards** – eg American Express, Diners Club – not really credit, because you have to pay off what you owe each month. However, you may be able to use your charge card to borrow money.

**WORTH CONSIDERING**

**Bank personal loan** – the money is paid into your current account; you make regular repayments. Less flexible than a bank ordinary loan. Quick and easy, but can be pricey.
APR 16% to 24% (fixed).
Usually quick and easy to arrange; no arrangement fee
BUT usual maximum 5 to 7 years; maximum loan £5,000 to £7,000.

**Home improvement loan** – available from some banks, building societies and finance companies. Cost varies widely – you could also consider increasing your mortgage (see opposite).
APR 13 to 24% (variable).
You may be able to borrow up to £30,000 for as long as 30 years. You may be able to get tax relief (see p247)
BUT available only for home improvements; you may need security; may not be able to borrow 100% of cost of improvements.

**BEST AVOIDED**

**Unauthorised overdraft** – going into the red on your current account without arranging it with your bank manager beforehand (see 'Bank overdraft', above and *Bank charges Update*).
APR 25% or more (variable). Bank charges will increase the cost further. Very expensive. You'll almost certainly have to pay bank charges. You're likely to have cheques bounced – which will cost you, too – and it will make you very unpopular with your bank.

**Trading checks** – you buy a check from a trading check company and pay for it in instalments. It's valid at any one of a list of shops.
APR 60% or more (fixed).
Very expensive. The shops on the list may not be the cheapest.

**Moneylenders** – make unsecured and sometimes secured loans and usually collect repayments door-to-door.
APR 60% to 1,000% (may be fixed or variable).
May lend to you even if you can't borrow elsewhere
BUT because they specialise in high-risk lending, they can be *extremely* expensive.

(APR = annual percentage rate)

O8     **Write a letter to a friend who knows little about the problems of borrowing money and who now needs about £8,000 to set up his/her own recording studio. He/She has asked for your advice. Using the information above, summarise the sorts of loan he/she might consider, point out some of the pitfalls, and recommend one.**

*A1*     **Look at this sentence and read it aloud to a partner:**

> Can we really attribute a 15% increase in the price of a 5lb bag of sugar
> from £1.60 to £1.84 to the agricultural policy of the EEC?

**What are some of the problems in reading aloud a sentence like the one above?**
**Discuss these questions with a partner:**

1 Was the sentence a statement or a question? What difference does that make to the way you read it?
2 Where would you breathe when reading the sentence?
3 Did you have difficulty in pronouncing any of the words – apart from figures and abbreviations? What about 'attribute', 'agricultural' and 'policy'?
4 How did you pronounce these: 15%? a 5 lb bag? £1.60? £1.84? EEC?
5 The phrase 'a 5 lb bag of sugar' contains two problems. Firstly, 'lb' is an abbreviation for 'pound' or 'pounds' (weight): how is it pronounced here – 'pound' or 'pounds'? And secondly, how do we pronounce 'of' in the phrase 'bag of sugar'?
6 How did you pronounce the words underlined in these phrases: 'in the price of a'? 'bag of sugar'? 'to the agricultural policy of the EEC'?

**Now listen to the sentence on cassette and try to imitate it.**

*A2*     **Here are a number of figures and abbreviations. Can you say them?**

| | | | | | | | |
|---|---|---|---|---|---|---|---|
| 13 | £1 | 0.25 | $\frac{1}{4}$ in | 2 in | 10% | | US$ 35 |
| 30 | £5 | 0.33 | $\frac{1}{3}$ cm | 60 cm | 13.75% | | FF 16,000 |
| 313 | .75p | 0.5 | $\frac{1}{2}$ m | 50 m | 13 x 15 | | DM 15,500 |
| 3,113 | £440.13(p) | 0.75 | $\frac{3}{4}$ kg | 13 oz | 40 ÷ 4 | | Dkr 13,000 |
| 400,000 | £16 m | 15.5 | 1 lb | 16 kg | 40 – 14 = 26 | | Esc. 14,000 |
| 50,000,000 | £4$\frac{1}{2}$ b | 0.09 | 1 ft | 20 yds | 16 + 40 = 56 | | 250,000 pts |

| | | | | | | |
|---|---|---|---|---|---|---|
| EEC | CBI | UFO | USSR | USA | UK | TWA |
| UNICEF | ICI | PLO | BBC | NATO | IMF | OXFAM |

**Listen to the figures and abbreviations on cassette, then practise them again.**

**Now read out these sentences concentrating on the figures and abbreviations:**

1 It's 1.5 m long and weighs 24 kg.
2 I spent about £1,500 in the USA.
3 The box measures 2 in x 3 in: that's about 5 cm x 7.5 cm.
4 The FBI and the CIA don't agree.
5 The headquarters of the CBI cost £1.5 m.
6 The man said the UFO was 50 m across.
7 We made DM3 m this year: that's 15% up on last year.
8 When it's 2.30 am here, it's 8.30 pm there.

Listen to the sentences on cassette and repeat them.

*A3*   **Read these sentences silently and think about how you would pronounce the words printed in bold. (Note: the words in bold do not necessarily indicate stress.)**

He earns a lot **of** money.
He wants **to** be a millionaire.
She's **at** the bank.
He borrowed it **from** his father.
This is the dress **that** I bought.
You know **them**, don't you?
She **was** ill when I saw her.
I'**d**/I **had** never been there before.

What's it made **of**?
It's time **to** eat, isn't it?
Who are you looking **at**?
Where does she come **from**?
What do you think of **that**?
What does the word '**them**' refer to?
Were you there? Yes, I **was**.
Had he booked the table? Yes, he **had**.

**Now listen to the sentences on cassette and repeat them.**

*A4*   **Study this dialogue and be prepared to read it aloud with a partner. Concentrate on preparing the Quizmaster's part. Think carefully about how you will say figures, letters and abbreviations, and prepositions like *of, at* and *to*.**

QUIZMASTER: Now here's Mr G.J. Johns from Stratford-upon-Avon, who...
MR JOHNS: Sorry, it's er J.K. Johns actually.
QUIZMASTER: I'm very sorry, Mr Johns. J.K. Johns. You need to get four out of the next six questions right to qualify for this week's star prize: the 14-day Mediterranean cruise, all expenses paid, plus £500 spending money. Now are you ready, Mr Johns?
MR JOHNS: Er, well, yes, as ready as I'll ever be.
QUIZMASTER: Right. Your first question, for 250 points. What is the capital of Hungary? Is it a) Belgrade? b) Bucharest? or c) Budapest?
MR JOHNS: Er, I think it's Budapest.
QUIZMASTER: And you're quite right. You have 215 points.
MR JOHNS: Only 215?
QUIZMASTER: My mistake. 250. And to put that up to 500, tell me: How many millimetres are there in a metre? Is is 100, 1,000 or 10,000?
MR JOHNS: Er, a thousand.
QUIZMASTER: You have 500 points. Now, what do the letters U.F.O. stand for?
MR JOHNS: Is it 'united freedom organisation'?
QUIZMASTER: I'm sorry, Mr Johns. U.F.O. (or UFO) stands for an 'unidentified flying object'.
MR JOHNS: Oh, yes, of course.
QUIZMASTER: Still, you have three more questions. In 1943 an American car costing $250,000 was used to drive a U.S. President. Was it a Rolls Royce, a Lincoln, or a Skoda?
MR JOHNS: Oh, I'll have a guess. A Lincoln.
QUIZMASTER: Quite right, it was a Lincoln Continental. Two questions to go. Can you spell 'career'?
MR JOHNS: Um er 'c-a-double r-i-e-r'.
QUIZMASTER: No, I'm sorry. There's only one 'r' and it's double 'e', not 'i-e': 'c-a-r-e-e-r'. And now your final question, Mr Johns, ...

**Read the dialogue with a partner twice. Take it in turns to read the Quizmaster's part.**

**Listen to the dialogue on cassette and try to copy the Quizmaster's part.**

# <sup>U N I T</sup>3 Entertainment

## *WARM-UP*

**Here is a list of different kinds of entertainment. Which do you like most and which don't you like at all? Re-order them according to your own preferences and write a numbered list. Discuss your order with a partner or small group.**

> the circus    ballet    the theatre    television    museums
> concerts (classical, pop or jazz)    the cinema    opera    art galleries

*A1*    **Look at this picture story and then do exercises** A2-A5**:**

*A2*    **Work in pairs, look at the pictures, and ask and answer questions like these.**

Pictures 1 and 2:  What are Peter and Maria doing (or what does it look as if they're doing)? Where are they? What is the poster advertising? How do you think they feel? Why do you think they feel like that? e.g. What tells you that they're [excited]?

*A3*    **Now, what about the tenses you need to tell a story like this in the past? As well as other tenses, you will need the *simple past* (walked, saw, bought, waited, etc.), the *continuous past* (were walking, was waiting, were wearing, etc.) and the *past perfect* (had bought, had missed, had wanted, etc.). You will also need joining words like these: *when, while, as soon as, before, after*, etc. - and words like these: *Next*, ...; *Then* ...; *However*, ..., etc.**

**Work in pairs, look at the pictures, and make sentences like these.**

Picture 1:  One day last month Peter and Maria were walking along the High Street when they saw an advertisement for a rock concert.

*A4*    **You will need other joining words, too, such as *because, although, since, so*, etc. Make a list of words like this you might need. Then again make sentences with some of the words for each picture. Here is an example:**

Picture 2:  Maria was very excited because she had always wanted to see 'Triangular Beat' live.

*A5*    **Now listen to the story on cassette. Listen particularly to the way the story-teller uses tenses and to the way she joins her ideas. Listen to it two or three times. When you feel ready, tell the story from the pictures yourself beginning with these words: 'One day last month Peter and Maria ...'**
**(You could tell the story in pairs, taking it in turns, one sentence each. Or you could tell it round the class.)**

*A6*    **In the exam you will have to do short 'grammar' exercises based on the picture story. First work with a partner and put the verbs in brackets in these sentences in the correct form – *do, to do* or *doing*.**

1 I enjoy (go) to the ballet.
2 I'd like (see) that new film.
3 She hates (visit) museums.
4 The children love (watch) ice hockey on TV.
5 I can't stand (listen) to pop music but I don't mind (listen) to jazz.
6 My parents would never let me (go) to a pop concert.
7 We'd better (get) there early.
8 We look forward to (go) to the theatre every Saturday evening.
9 I insist on (buy) the best seats.
10 It isn't necessary (book), is it?

*A7*    **Now listen to the cassette and do the same kind of thing. You will hear some sentences about the story and you must complete them, using the right form of the phrase 'sing with the group'.**

*01*   **Dictionary work**

**As preparation for the tasks on the next four pages, use your English-English dictionary to do these exercises (in pairs or individually):**

1  Magazines and newspapers contain résumés and reviews of films, plays and so on. What is the difference between a *résumé* and a *review* ?
2  Most films have a producer and a director. What does a film *producer* do? What does a film *director* do?
3  Explain the difference between *set* and *shot* in this sentence:
    'The film was set in India: it was shot in Spain.'
4  What does each of these people do: *a viewer, a cinema-goer, a theatre-goer*?
5  Explain, and write example sentences using, the verbs *amuse* and *entertain*, and the nouns *amusement* and *entertainment* .
6  The following words and phrases all have something to do with the theatre or the cinema. What do they mean? Work in A/B pairs: look them up and explain to each other.
    A: on location;  a box-office hit;  on the screen;  an act (2 meanings);
    B: a variety show;  the climax;  a floor show;  cabaret;  the dénouement
7  Each of these words describes a special kind of (stage) play or film. Explain them and give an example:
    a tragedy;  a comedy;  a farce;  a kitchen-sink drama;  a melodrama

*02*   **This kind of writing task might appear in an Oxford Higher Paper 1:**

> 'As part of a page of film reviews for an English-language magazine in your own country, you have been asked to write a brief résumé of a film you have seen recently. Write the résumé.' (About 200-250 words.)

**How do you go about it? Opposite is an example (in about 200 words) of just such a résumé. Read it carefully, then answer or discuss the questions below.**

1  What do you notice about the tenses used in the résumé?
2  How many characters are mentioned in the résumé? Why are no other characters mentioned, do you think?
3  There are three paragraphs. What does each do?
4  The very last two lines are printed in italics. What's special about them? What do they do?

*03*   **Now cover the résumé of *The Cassandra Crossing* and write the first two paragraphs of it again. Use these notes as prompts:**

■ start – young terrorist – wounded – infected – abortive attack – laboratory – WHA – Geneva
■ boards express
■ man must be found: authorities – dilemma:  search train – continue route – risk infecting?  send passengers – isolation camp – Cassandra Crossing?

*04*   **If you are asked to write a *review* of a book, a film or a play, you should not only give a brief résumé of the story: you will also be expected to give your opinion and then a recommendation – as in the boxed sentence below the film résumé opposite.**
**Write the review of a film for a magazine. Use the following points and questions to make notes. Then write the review in about 250 words. Work alone or with a partner.**

1 Decide which film you are going to review.
2 How would you describe the kind of film? Is it a Western, a sci-fi (science fiction), a historical drama, a war film, a comedy, a thriller, a farce, a spy film, a mystery, a horror film, a love story, or ...?
3 What happens in the film? i.e. What's the storyline? Make a few notes or even one simple sentence to summarise it, for example: 'The Good Doctor tracks down the evil vampire and destroys him.'
4 Write brief notes to tell the story in more detail: put them in paragraphs and begin to draft the résumé (in the present simple).
5 If you can, add a sentence which summarises the 'essence' of the film.
6 Give your opinion of the film and a recommendation to your readers.

## The Cassandra Crossing

At the start of the film *The Cassandra Crossing* a young terrorist, wounded and infected with a deadly virus (plague), escapes from an abortive attack on a laboratory in the World Health Authority building in Geneva. Unnoticed, he manages to board the trans-continental Geneva-to-Stockholm express.

The man *must* be found, but the authorities are faced with an awful dilemma: do they search the train while it continues its route, stopping and starting to let people on and off, but risk the man infecting millions? Or do they seal the train, re-route it and send the 1,000 passengers to an isolation camp which lies the other side of the highly dangerous railway bridge called the Cassandra Crossing?

Dr Chamberlain, played by Richard Harris, is the doctor-hero on the train who treats any infected passengers. The American Col. Mackenzie, played by Burt Lancaster, controls the destiny of the express and its occupants from his office in Geneva.

*The morality of germ warfare research is questioned, our suspicions of military authority are aroused, and our faith in the basic goodness of human nature is confirmed.*

This is a thoroughly enjoyable action-packed thriller which I would recommend to anyone looking for intrigue, excitement and suspense.

*O5*   **You see this advertisement in an old newspaper and realise you've missed the exhibition. You would very much like to have seen it.**

**Write two letters:**

1  to the museum asking if there is a catalogue still available, whether the exhibition is coming to your country, and if so, when, where it will be shown, etc.

2  to a friend who you remember went to see the exhibition, asking him or her about it.

**Use these notes and questions:**

1  Will your letters be formal or informal?
2  So where will you write your address? Who will you address the letter to? And how will you begin the two letters?
3  Which letter will be shorter? The shorter letter will probably have two paragraphs. What will you say in each? The longer letter might have three or four paragraphs. What will you say in each?
4  How will you end the letters?
5  How will the style of the two letters differ?

*O6*   **The small ads opposite appeared in the Arts and Entertainments Guide of *The Guardian* newspaper. Study them and do the following exercises.**

1  Imagine you are staying in London and would like to go to the theatre with a friend this evening.

a)  Which play (or plays) would it be very difficult to get tickets for?
b)  Which plays should you be able to get seats for with little difficulty?

## Theatre

(A) Seats at all prices.
(S) Limited availability.
(R) Returns only.
(D) Disabled access.

● **BARTHOLOMEW FAIR**
Ben Jonson's rollicking comedy, in a production by Richard Eyre.
**National Theatre: Olivier** South Bank SE1 (01-928 2252) 7.15, £6.50-£14, (D) Tube/BR: Waterloo. (S)

● **ELECTRA**
Extraordinary production of Sophocles' tragedy by Deborah Warner, with a raw, powerfully desperate Fiona Shaw in the title role.
**The Pit** Barbican Centre EC2 (01-638 8891) 7.30, Thur & Sat 2.00 & 7.30, £8.50. Tube: Barbican/Moorgate. (R)

● **HENCEFORWARD**
Ayckbourn takes farce into a non-user-friendly future, where composer Jerome (Ian McKellen) struggles to get over a three-year creative block. Jane Asher plays his estranged wife.
**Vaudeville Theatre** Strand WC2 (01-836 9987/5645) 7.30, Sat 5.00 & 8.30, Wed mat 2.30, £7.50-£15. Tube/BR: Charing Cross. (S)

● **LETTICE AND LOVAGE**
Geraldine McEwan takes over from Maggie Smith in Peter Shaffer's delightfully dotty comedy. Also now with Sara Kestelman.
**Globe Theatre** Shaftesbury Avenue W1 (01-437 3667/cc 741 9999) 7.45, Sat 3.00 & 7.45, £7.50-£15. (D) Tube: Piccadilly Circus. (S)

● **MAKING HISTORY**
Brian Friel's new play examining the life and times of the English educated Earl of Tyrone, and his war against Elizabeth I.
**National Theatre: Cottesloe** South Bank SE1 (01-928 2252) 7.30, Tue & Sat 2.30 & 7.30, £7.50. (D) Tube/BR: Waterloo. (R)

● **A MAN WITH CONNECTIONS**
Powerful two-hander from contemporary Soviet playwright Aleksandr Gelman. Bill Paterson plays an ambitious site-manager cutting corners with tragic results. Marty Cruikshank is his not entirely blameless wife.
**Royal Court Theatre** Sloane Square SW1 (01-730 1745/cc 836 25428) 8.00, £4-£12. Tube: Sloane Square. (A)

● **MRS KLEIN**
The human failings and foibles of child psychoanalyst Melanie Klein, here played by Gillian Barge. Francesca Annis plays her estranged daughter. Also with Zoe Wanamaker.
**Apollo Theatre** Shaftesbury Avenue W1 (01-437 2663/4) 8.00, Sat 4.30 & 8.00, £5-£14.50. Tube: Piccadilly Circus. (S)

● **ORPHEUS DESCENDING**
Jean-Marc Barr plays the charismatic and oracular Val, who descends into the bigoted hell of small-town Southern America in Tennessee Williams's play. Vanessa Redgrave is immensely powerful as Lady.

**Haymarket Theatre** Haymarket SW1 (01-930 9832) 7.30, Thur & Sat 2.30 & 7.30, £4-£15. (D) Tube: Piccadilly Circus/Charing Cross. (S)

● **RICHARD III**
Derek Jacobi follows on from his strong interpretation of Richard II, to tackle the darker nature of Richard III.
**Phoenix** Charing Cross Road WC2 (01-240 9661/2/cc 836 2294) 7.30 (Jan 19 at 7.00), £6-£14.50. Tube: Leicester Square/Tottenham Court Road. (S)

● **THREE SISTERS**
Harriet Walter is wonderfully nervy, caged Masha in John Barton's enlightening production. Brian Cox plays Vershinin.
**Barbican Theatre** Barbican Centre EC2 (01-638 8891) 7.30, £5-£15. (D) Tube: Barbican/Moorgate. (S)

● **A WALK IN THE WOODS**
A nice but unspectacular script is winningly redeemed by fine performances from Alec Guinness and his co-star Edward Herrmann in Lee Blessing's arms negotiations play. Ronald Eyre directs.
**Comedy Theatre** Panton Street SW1 (01-930 2578/cc 839 1438) 8.00, Wed 3.00 & 8.00, Sat 4.00 & 8.00, £4-£16. (D) Tube: Piccadilly Circus/Leicester Square. (S)

**2** Work with a partner and use a dictionary to explain these words and expressions as they are used in the ads:

1 rollicking ('Bartholomew Fair')
2 block ('Henceforward')
3 estranged ('Henceforward' and 'Mrs Klein')
4 dotty ('Lettice and Lovage')
5 foibles ('Mrs Klein')
6 charismatic ('Orpheus Descending')
7 bigoted ('Orpheus Descending')
8 enlightening ('Three Sisters')

**3** Which actors, actresses or directors/producers receive clear compliments for their work in these plays? And which reviews, if any, contain some words of criticism?

*O7* **You're studying in an international school. The school is putting on a show, a drama evening or an evening of music, folksongs, etc. with refreshments, and you have been asked to organise the publicity. Compose a small advertisement in not more than 20-30 words to go into a local newspaper. How do you go about it?**

# UNIT 4 Alternatives

## WARM-UP

**In pairs, in groups or as a class, quickly suggest some alternatives to:**

- wearing fur
- electricity produced by nuclear energy
- the motor car
- working for a living
- normal office working hours
- saving money in a bank
- watching television every evening

O1  **Without looking up any words you do not know, read the article opposite quickly, then:**

1 Make up *your own* headline for the article.
2 Tell a partner what you think of the article, and briefly explain why.

O2  **Dictionary work**

**Read the article again and list any words you don't know and can't really deduce the meanings of. Compare your list with other students'. You will probably all have different lists: explain to each other any words that you can. Only then should you consult your dictionary for any common difficulties.**

O3  **Now read the article carefully and use the information to answer the following questions. Instead of giving your answers in complete sentences, you can give them in note form, provided you make your meaning clear. Where you are asked to say whether a statement is True or False, give reasons.**

1 Jean Bendell is one of some 10,000 parents in Britain who have decided to do – what?
2 What is *School's Out*? And can you explain why it is quite a clever title?
3 What kind of an education did Mrs Bendell have herself?
4 What was the main reason for the Bendells deciding to educate their children at home?
5 What Mrs Bendell is doing is illegal under the 1944 Education Act. True or False?
6 Instead of talking about 'educating her children', Mrs Bendell talks about 'facilitating their education'. Why?
7 The visiting primary school adviser has said Mrs Bendell has become increasingly complimentary about the children's achievements. True or False?
8 How would you summarise Jean Bendell's philosophy of education?
9 What do you think she means when she says that 'they [the children] have to be self-propelling to a great extent'?
10 Mrs Bendell tends to play down educational qualifications. What does she think is more important?

And one last question: Would you buy her book? Why?/Why not?

# No place like home for going to school

JEAN BENDELL chooses to teach her children at home rather than leave their education in the hands of a school.

She is one of a growing number of British parents – perhaps as many as 10,000 – who are opting to educate their offspring outside the formal education system.

Mrs Bendell, aged 35, lives on a housing estate on the southern edge of Bath with her husband, Victor, aged 53, and their daughters, 11-year-old Hosanna ("the name came to me in a dream"), five-year-old Fiorin, an Irish name for wild grass which also means "the Fairy folk", an Irish name for wild grass which also means "the Fairy folk", and five-month-old son, Taliesin, named after a Welsh bard.

Next Monday sees the publication of *School's Out*, an autobiographical account of how and why she decided to teach her children at home.

An earth mother figure in floral print dress with a taste for words such as "unstructured," "facilitate" and "meaningful", Mrs Bendell is a sometime art student with a "reasonable number of O-levels ... more than five", an A-level in English and a passionate interest in poetry. A born romantic, she left her Islington grammar school at

16 to elope with the man who was later to become her husband.

"Our major reason for not sending our children to school," she says in the book, was "what we call poetic awareness in life rather than specifically in literature. We felt this sense of wonder at the world would be lost very quickly with constant exposure to the routine of the classroom. We did not want our children to be engulfed by a mediocre, mass culture".

She recalls unhappy experiences with nursery schools and playgroups. "What really struck me was that I was forever having to take Hosanna away from things that were interesting and meaningful ... a book, a snail trail gleaming in the sunlight, moss growing on a wall ... and put her into an environment where things were set out in a structured way," she says.

When Hosanna was four, Mrs Bendell met another mum who belonged to a pressure group called Education Otherwise, which advises parents of their rights under the 1944 Education Act to have their

children educated "either by regular attendance at school or otherwise".

Mrs Bendell chose otherwise. Today, after initial hostility from the local education authority, she "facilitates" her daughters' education at home by way of informal conversations and more formal "school work" sessions in the kitchen and bedroom. These tend to take place in the mornings, after the dog and rabbits have been fed and watered.

She feels that the family can cope with primary education – reading, writing and mathematics – and that secondary schooling will be challenging. The Bendells consider that their reasonably broad spread of interests should be sufficient to prepare the children for up to 10 GCSE subjects and the children can always use correspondence courses, take part-time classes at local colleges and draw on the skills and expertise of their friends. Every now and then, the children are visited by the education authority's primary school adviser who, says Mrs Bendell, has become increasingly complimentary about their

achievements.

"Educating children," she says "is not filling them up with facts and figures. I see it very much as drawing out their interests and abilities. I think that the absolute strength of home education is that it gives the child an education that is very rich in ideas, and enables them to grasp concepts very easily".

"When it gets to a certain point the children will have to take on the responsibility for learning themselves. Obviously I could not coach a child through GCSEs and do it all for her and another child and another child. They have to be self-propelling to a great extent.

"We felt: 'why was there a magic age when you needed experts to educate the children?'. Although the teachers may be better qualified to teach individual subjects than I am, what if the children in those classes are spending the time doodling and looking out of the window? What real use are those history or geography degrees? It is the learning the child does for himself that actually makes the difference."

"Educational qualifications will be picked up I hope somewhere along the way," she says. "They might be useful to the children. Happiness is the important thing. You can be a successful nursery nurse without doing lots of A-levels, you can be a successful window cleaner. I would be disappointed if I had failed to equip the children to do what they wanted to do."

At the moment Fiorin wants to be a vet, Hosanna a doctor.

■ *School's Out. Educating Your Child At Home* by Jean Bendell is published by the Ashgrove Press on Monday at £4.95.

**Simon Midgley**

04  **A friend who is studying for a degree in Education at a foreign university has written to you in English to ask if you can help with some research. He/She has been asked to investigate and report on the findings of any experiments into alternative forms of education. You recently came across the article on page 27 in a newspaper. Write and tell your friend about it. (About 250 words).**

Use these points and questions to write the letter:

1  Where are you writing from? What date is it? Who are you writing to?
2  Paragraph 1: Begin with some 'polite noises': Nice to hear from you ... , etc.
3  Paragraph 2 (and 3?): Answer the point of his/her letter: quote title of article (it's from *The Independent* newspaper): explain what it's about. Summarise 2-3 advantages and disadvantages. Recommend Jean Bendell's book.
4  Decide how to close the letter.

05  **You have been looking for a full-time course in business administration and spotted this advertisement in the newspaper.**
**Read it carefully. You can't attend the reception, so you decide to write for further information. (About 50 words)**

**Below is a brave attempt at the letter, but it's not very good. Can you improve on it? Write your (politer, more formal) version complete with addresses, etc.**

Manchester Business School
University of Manchester

THE RIGHT COURSE OF ACTION

The MBS Master's Degree in Business Administration has long been internationally acclaimed for its action-based approach to management education. As a graduate of the course you'll have vastly greater career flexibility. And you'll be an outstanding candidate for rapid promotion in both public and private sectors.

If you'd like to talk informally to MBS staff about how the course could enhance your career, come along to our reception at:

Randolph Hotel (Worcester Room),
1, Beaumont Street, Oxford.
Monday 24th October. 4.30pm-7.00pm.

If you can't attend, but would like more details contact the Graduate Office at:
Manchester Business School, Booth Street West, Manchester M15 6PB. Tel: 061-273 8228 Ext. 324

THE MANCHESTER MBA

---

Dear Mr _____ or Mrs _____ ,

I saw your advertisement in yesterday's 'Oxford Mail' for courses towards the MBS Master's Degree in Business Administration.

I can't go to the reception on 24th October, so could you send me some more information?

I shall look out for your letter.

Yours sincerely,

O6   **While in England, you receive a letter from a friend who is studying English abroad. Since receiving the letter, you have come across a Guide to some serious English magazines (below). Read this part of the friend's letter and answer it (in about 150 words) using the information in the Guide. But first discuss in pairs how to approach this task.**

> I'll be leaving college next year. Naturally I want to keep up my English, so I thought it would be a good idea if I read an English magazine regularly. I wonder if you could give me some advice on which good British magazine(s) I should read from time to time. I hope to be working in television, so obviously I'd be interested in anything to do with the media. You know too that I'm interested in politics, literature and the theatre, and world environmental problems. And I enjoy a good laugh — especially anything satirical! Perhaps you can recommend 2-3 different magazines.

# Which magazine?

| Magazines \ Features | Finance/Economics | Politics | Law & Order/Crime | Environment | Science, Technology | Current affairs | Industrial/Trades unions | Health and Social welfare | Royal family/Other celebrities | Humour & Satire | Arts, TV, radio | Literature, Theatre | Foreign affairs, news & comment |
|---|---|---|---|---|---|---|---|---|---|---|---|---|---|
| The Listener | ● | ● | | | | | | | | ● | ● | ● | |
| New Scientist | | | | ● | ● | | | ● | | | | | ● |
| The Economist | ● | ● | | | ● | ● | ● | | | | | ● | ● |
| New Statesman and Society | ● | ● | ● | | | ● | | ● | | | ● | ● | |
| Illustrated London News | ● | | | ● | | ● | | | ● | | ● | ● | ● |
| Punch | ● | ● | | | | ● | | | | ● | ● | ● | |

● a feature which appears frequently in the magazine

*A1*　**Giving a short persuasive talk on a prepared topic**
**Here are six typical topics for ARELS Higher persuasive talks. Decide quickly which one you could talk about right now.**

1　'Dangerous sports such as mountain-climbing and hang-gliding should be more controlled.'
2　'Modern popular music is getting worse every year.'
3　'The cinema is for entertainment: television should be educational.'
4　'Money put away and not used is wasted.'
5　'Professional sportsmen and women are too well paid.'
6　'Cycling, walking and swimming are the three best forms of exercise.'

*A2*　**Choosing and preparing a topic**
Was it easy or quite difficult to make a quick decision in **A1**? Why?
Here are some questions you might ask yourself when faced with a choice of topics. Think about them and discuss them with a partner. Any other considerations?

1　Have I anything to say? Do I agree or disagree with the statement? Or doesn't the subject concern or interest me?
2　Have I got enough English to talk about the subject for 2 minutes?
3　Where shall I start? What points do I want to make in the middle? What conclusion do I want to draw?

*A3*　**Making notes**
**Let's say you've decided to talk about topic 6 because you've got something to say, it interests you, and you think your English is up to the task. Remember you can make notes, but there's no point in making masses of notes or in writing out complete sentences. Look at these: What do good notes consist of?**

| These are complete sentences, NOT notes! | Better! | Even better! |
|---|---|---|
| 1　First of all, I must say that I think cycling is an excellent sport. | 1　must say – cycling – excellent sport | 1　cycling – excellent sport |
| 2　I've been riding a bicycle regularly since I was six years old. | 2　I – ride bicycle – regularly since I was six | 2　riding bike – since six |

**Here are some sentences you might say in a talk. Write out the ideas in note form, then give your notes to a partner to see if he or she could make sentences from them.**

1　There's no doubt that of all the media, television exerts the greatest influence on the lives of a large percentage of the population.
2　In my opinion, the only realistic alternatives to nuclear power are tidal ....
3　It seems an obvious thing to say, but hang-gliders use air space which may also be used by powered aircraft, large and small.
4　Most experts on health and physical exercise agree that, whatever your age, regular swimming is one of the best and most enjoyable ways of keeping fit.
5　The trouble with modern pop music is that so much of it sounds the same.

**Now write some points you would make for a talk on topic 6.**

*A4*    **Giving your talk**

In the exam, your talk is marked mainly for its interest, relevance, persuasiveness and fluency, and less for accuracy of language. Perhaps the best approach is to imagine you are talking to a friend, trying to persuade him/her of the truth and logic of your opinions. So how formal or informal do you think your talk should be?

*A5*    **1**  Here are the notes someone made for a talk on topic 5 (A1). Look at them as you listen to his talk. (Remember you can agree or disagree with the topic.)

> – prof. sportsmen / women not overpaid
> – highly professional – skilled – talented – result of years of practice / training : personal sacrifices
> – e.g. top athletes – hours practising and training
> – can't compare prof. sportsmen / women with ord. jobs
> – prof. sportsmen = entertainers, therefore should earn same
> – teaching, coaching, lecturing
> – many – short professional life – retire at 30 ?

**2**  Listen carefully to the talk again. What language did he use to indicate that he was going to, or was about to

    1  make a new point?    3  give his own opinion?    5  make a comparison?
    2  give an example?      4  put another point of view?  6  finish his talk?

What language might he have used to
1  list points?    2  remind his listener(s) of something?    3  correct himself?

*A6*    Look at the topics in A1 again. Choose one, spend 5 minutes preparing what you want to say, then give a two-minute talk on it (to a small group or the class).

*A7*    **And now for something different ...**

It's not only the words we use in English that convey a message. It's also the way we say things – the intonation we use. The sentence 'I don't eat raw vegetables very often myself' is repeated on cassette a number of times: the words and grammar are exactly the same, but it is said in a different way each time. Repeat each one and then complete it as appropriate. Here is an example: the words in bold show which words are stressed.

You hear:  **I** don't eat raw vegetables very often **myself**, ...
You say:   **I** don't eat raw vegetables very often **myself**, but my **parents** do.

*A8*    **And what about offering alternatives? Listen to (and repeat) the different ways we can make offers of alternatives. Then offer a partner these alternatives:**

    1  a sandwich / a piece of cake       4  go to the exhibition / go sailing
    2  buy her a present / give her a     5  steak and chips / spaghetti bolognese
       gift token                         6  watch the programme now / record it
    3  water / lemonade                          for later

# UNIT 5 People

## WARM-UP

**Imagine you were organising a similar event in your own town or city to the one described right. Make a list of ten people (actors? singers? pop stars? politicians? sportmen/sportswomen?) you would invite to take part. Then explain and justify your choices in small groups.**

On Saturday July 30, 1988, nearly 200 well-known faces were to be seen serving in stores, bars and restaurants in the Covent Garden area of London. It was all part of a charity event in which celebrities gave up their time to raise money for AIDS sufferers. In this way, 'Shop Assistance', the name given to the scheme, aimed to increase the customary million or so Saturday shoppers in the area by 50% and make over £100,000 profit. All participating establishments gave 5% of their day's (much-increased) takings.

### A1    Situational responses

When you respond to a situation in the exam, it might be necessary to use two, or even three short sentences. For example:

a) You state your problem and then ask for help:
    'I'm having a bit of trouble with this window. Do you think you could hold it open while I push this piece of wood under here?'
b) You comment on someone's apparent difficulty and then offer help:
    'You look as if you could do with some help. Would you like me to push the car for you, while you try to start it.'
c) You apologise, criticise yourself and promise to make amends:
    'I'm terribly sorry about that record of yours. It was really very careless of me. Look, I'll get you another copy first thing Monday morning.'

**Give a two- or three-sentence response to these situations, using the starters:**

| | | |
|---|---|---|
| 1 You see a friend doing his homework with a worried frown on his face. What do you say to him? | (Comment) (Offer help) | *You seem ...* *Would you like ...?* |
| 2 You see two young boys playing football in a busy street. What do you say? | (Criticise) (Point out danger) | *You really shouldn't ...* *You wouldn't stand a chance if ...* |
| 3 A colleague has just given you a garment as a present for your new baby. What do you say? | (Thank) (Enthuse) (Repeat thanks) | *Thank ...* *It's ...* *It was very ... but you really shouldn't ...* |
| 4 A good friend has just passed a very important examination. What do you say to her? | (Congratulate) (Empathise) (Flatter) | *Congratulations on ...* *You must be ...* *I always knew ...* |
| 5 A music cassette you bought last week is blank on one side. What do you say when you take it back to the shop? | (Explain) (Request) | *I bought ... and when I got home, I ...* *Could you ...?* |

🖭 **Now respond to some more situations on the tape.**

## A2    Listening to a recorded interview

Section 3 of the ARELS Higher always includes part of a real interview for listening comprehension. You will hear it twice. The first time it is played in its entirety for you to get used to the speakers' voices and for you to understand the gist of what is said. The second time you hear it, the interview is frequently interrupted and you are asked questions to which you must give spoken answers.

**1  Listen to the interview once and answer these questions briefly:**

1  What does Peter do?
2  What are some of the things his job entails?

**2  Now listen to the interview again. This time try to answer the questions on tape.**

## A3

Sometimes in the ARELS exam you have to listen to short pieces of conversation and answer just one question. You may simply have to identify the speaker, or decide where he/she is, or what he/she is doing. In this exercise you must deduce the speaker's profession. Here is a written example.

> I suppose my hours are divided more or less equally between time on the beat and time spent at the station. I can tell you it's not all the glamour of high-speed car chases and dramatic arrests, oh no. Masses of paperwork, lost cats, lost umbrellas. Here we probably only charge five or six people a day, if that.

What's this person's job? How many clues are there in what he says? Put a ring around them. What's the problem with words like *station* and *charge*?

Now listen to four people speaking on the tape. Look at the nine jobs below. Write 1, 2, 3 and 4 in the boxes beside the four people according to the order in which you hear them. Then listen again and note down the clues which led you to those decisions. Compare your list of clues – and solutions – with a partner's.

| | | | |
|---|---|---|---|
| gardener ☐ | mechanic ☐ | nurse ☐ |
| butcher ☐ | journalist ☐ | bank cashier ☐ |
| air-hostess ☐ | piano tuner ☐ | car salesman ☐ |

## A4    Listening and summarising

**1  Listen to an Ansaphone message on tape. In the examination, you may have to summarise something like this in a very short time. There is a lot of information in the message, so decide first whether the words and phrases below are vital or could be omitted. Underline those that are crucial.**

| | | | | |
|---|---|---|---|---|
| Schmidt | gone 7 | clients from Edinburgh | 18.06 | S–C–H. |
| 16.45 | station | Johnsons | six months | |

What other vital information do you hear?

**2  Now listen to someone summarising the message in 30 seconds. Then you try.**

<u>01</u>    **Look at these five greetings card messages. What do they refer to?**

| | | | |
|---|---|---|---|
| **BEST WISHES ON YOUR** *21*^ST | SORRY TO HEAR YOU'VE BEEN UNDER THE WEATHER | *Congratulations on the birth of your baby daughter* | **GOOD LUCK IN YOUR NEW HOME** |

*Wishing you a Happy Retirement*

**Here is a collection of personal messages which could be added to the above. Sort them out so that there are two for each. What differences do you notice in each pair?**

1  Enjoy your rest — you deserve it, mate. We'll miss you.
2  We hope your new neighbours will be as kind and thoughtful to you as you've been to us.
3  So when's the housewarming party?
4  Hoping your life will continue to be as successful as it has been till now.
5  With all good wishes for a speedy recovery.
6  Delighted to hear about your happy event. God bless all three of you.
7  Get well soon. We need you back in the team.
8  Seems like only yesterday you were in nappies. All the best for the future.
9  Enjoy the night-life!! Any thoughts about a name yet?
10  With sincere gratitude for your invaluable help over the years.

<u>02</u>    **Notice, among other things, that formal language relies heavily on nouns (*gratitude, recovery, event*) and well-chosen adjectives (*successful, thoughtful, speedy, enjoyable, sincere, invaluable*). Informal language abounds with verbs (*enjoy, deserve, seem, miss*).**

**Now write your own personal messages to follow the printed messages in these cards. Try to write with a suitable degree of formality.**

1    *Hearty Congratulations on your Twenty-fifth Wedding Anniversary*    (to your boss, whom you see twice a year)

2    Wishing you well in your new job    (a colleague with whom you get on very well)

3    **Sorry To Hear You Failed Your Driving Test**    (your 17-year-old cousin)

4    Congratulations on your *ENGAGEMENT*    (an old friend that you haven't seen for years)

5    **You've passed! Well done!**    (a good friend: music exam)

O3   1  Skim through the article in no more than 30 seconds and then discuss with your
        partner what you have understood from it so far.
     2  Read the article more carefully now. Then work with a partner to try and place the
        references below in context from memory. For example:

> 16. – That's how old the boy is.
>  7. – That's the number of passes he would have got in the old exam.

a) At primary school;  b) 8;  c) Sutherland Road, West Croydon;
d) English literature and craft;  e) English language;  f) Two years;
g) Dyslexia;  h) Westminster Children's Hospital;
i) At a plastics company;  j) Sweeping roads.

# GCSE triumph for dyslexic teenager

**By David Tytler**
**Education Editor**

Tony Shurmer and Mrs Gail Treml with a model car he built in his spare time (Photograph: Peter Trievnor).

A dyslexic boy aged 16 who was diagnosed as "subnormal" while at primary school celebrated GCSE results yesterday that would have given him seven passes in the old GCE O level examinations — and he still has a reading age of only eight.

Tony Shurmer took the examinations in a private room and dictated his answers to two teachers who read him the questions. In the technical examination he drew his own diagrams, with the teachers writing in the labels and captions on his instructions.

One of them, Mrs Gail Treml, the special needs co-ordinator at Lanfranc High School in Croydon, south-west London, said: "I did not understand a word of the physics paper and I disagreed with lots of his ideas and arguments in English Literature. But they were all his and his practical work was better than most."

Tony, of Sutherland Road, West Croydon, was awarded B grades in English literature and craft, design and technology; Cs in information technology, sociology, electronics, physics, and mathematics; and a D in English language.

It took Mrs Treml two years to persuade the examining groups to allow the boy to dictate his answers in the GCSE examinations, a method permitted in cases of physical disability.

The London borough of Croydon, which is taking the first steps in setting up a City Technology College with special facilities for dyslexic children, does not recognize dyslexia as a medical condition.

The borough's educational psychologists diagnosed Tony as having specific reading and writing difficulties. An examination at Westminster Children's Hospital confirmed he was dyslexic.

Throughout his GCSE courses either Mrs Treml or her assistant, Mrs Denise Duffin, sat in lessons, reading and writing for him.

Tapes of his GCSE answers were sent to the examiners with the written work.

Tony has been given an apprenticeship at a plastics company. He said yesterday: "Without Mrs Treml I would be sweeping roads".
● Mr Dennis Hatfield, chairman of the Joint Council for the GCSE, will today begin an investigation into allegations that grades had been "fixed" and that an unnamed examination board had decided to "massage" results.

GCSE = The General Certificate of Secondary Education, the examination for 15/16-year-olds which has replaced the former GCE 'O' (Ordinary) Level examination in England, Wales and Northern Ireland.

*04*    **This is part of a letter you have received from an acquaintance.**

> Everything's very much the same here. Bill's <u>counting</u> on some kind of promotion in the next few months; June says she might be <u>off</u> soon to get her own flat up in town and I'm, well, to tell the truth, I've been feeling a bit <u>low</u> lately. As usual, it's Eric who's giving us most <u>headaches</u>. He still doesn't seem to be getting anywhere with his schoolwork. It's all very well for the <u>head</u> to go on about how dyslexia is very common and it isn't <u>that</u> serious and we shouldn't think <u>twice</u> about it, but he's coming up to fourteen now and still has trouble with the most basic words. I'm at my wits' end, I am, sometimes. I dread to think what'll <u>become</u> of him when it comes to these GCSE exams they do nowadays.
>
> Anyway, mustn't let things get me <u>down</u>, I know. It's just that, as you know, we had such high hopes for him when he was younger; he seemed such a <u>bright thing</u>.

**The meaning of the words underlined above is not the first meaning you would find given in a dictionary. With the help of the latter, as and when you need it, work out what the words mean in these contexts and find synonyms.**

*05*    **Now write a reply to your depressed friend to try and cheer her up. Follow this plan:**

- Thank her for her letter
- Sympathise, but not too much, with regard to Eric's problem
- Mention the article on p. 35, which you saw in a newspaper recently
- Summarise the main points of the article – might this inspire Eric?
- Suggest she might take steps to get Eric treated as a special case in exams
- Tell her to keep her chin up and invite her to lunch one day.

*06*    **Opposite are snippets from five different sources about individuals and their money.**

1   Read the snippets and arrange them in pairs. (There are ten paragraphs from five different articles.) Decide which of each pair comes first. Then discuss how you made your decisions and what clues were available to you.

2   Here are three possible headlines for one of the articles. Which do you think is the most suitable? Why?

**PARENTS FIGHT ON FOR PROPER COMPENSATION**

**GIRL AWARDED NEARLY A MILLION FOR BRAIN DAMAGE**

**COURT AWARDS GIRL £800,000 DAMAGES**

1 The film has sold a <u>phenomenal</u> 15 million copies in America at a cost of $19.50 each, while in Britain <u>close to</u> 100,000 copies have been bought, and over three million sold throughout the rest of the world.

2 The award, one of the highest settlements for medical negligence, and agreed out of court, is the result of a <u>gruelling</u> battle by her parents to make the East Anglia, Cambridge and Huntingdon health authorities take responsibility for her injuries.

3 Sharon Head is not a lady to do things <u>by halves</u>. In a career of crime which lasted <u>a mere</u> four years, she committed 2,257 offences, stole 291 cars, <u>purloined</u> goods worth £1,136,062 – and when she was caught she <u>penned</u> a 37-page confession after talking to police for 165 hours.

4 Judge Martin Stephens, QC, told her at Cardiff Crown Court yesterday: "Your catalogue of crimes <u>almost defies belief</u>."

5 The Queen remains the world's richest woman and top of the list of 12 British dollar billionaire families, according to *Fortune* magazine. With property assets, racehorses, jewellery, art and stamp collections and "vast share-holdings", she is worth $8.7 billion (£5.1 billion).

6 In a fitting prelude to her new life as a billionairess, the richest three-year-old in the world was last week <u>secluded</u> behind a high-security fence, flanked by bodyguards, while lawyers circled around her fortune, <u>like vultures around their prey.</u>

7 Film Director Steven Spielberg has negotiated one of the most extraordinary deals in showbusiness. It will make him $100 million. It is the financial contract his lawyers drew up for video cassettes of his <u>blockbuster</u> classic ET. For each cassette that is sold Spielberg will receive a royalty of $5.

8 Like Marie Antoinette, Athina Onassis was playing with her own flock of sheep, complete with yodelling Swiss shepherd, and her £10,000 miniature Ferrari Testarossa – modelled on Don Johnson's in Miami Vice – safe from would-be kidnappers and the <u>prying</u> eyes of the world's press.

9 Three health authorities agreed yesterday to pay £800,000 damages to a 15-year-old who received <u>devastating</u> and <u>irreversible</u> brain damage as a result of a hospital <u>blunder</u> seven years ago.

10 She also earns $30 million a year, free of tax, from overseas investments, it said.

3 Look at the headlines opposite. What kind of words are omitted, and what tense is used to describe past events?
Write headlines for the other four articles. Then compare the merits of your headlines with those of your partners'.

4 Using your dictionary, replace the underlined words and phrases with your own substitutions. In which cases do you think your alternative is better than, just as good as, or less effective than the original?

# UNIT 6 Our Changing World

## WARM-UP

**Nearly everything in the world around us is changing, isn't it? Our lifestyles, certainly. Our attitudes. And, it seems, the amount of general knowledge people have to acquire. The article below summarises the results of a survey conducted in Britain in 1988 to test teachers' general knowledge. Before you read it, see if you can answer these five questions. Compare your answers with a partner's.**

1  What is 15% of £10?
2  What is the capital of Poland?
3  How many millimetres are there in a metre?
4  Who is Nelson Mandela?
5  How do you spell the word that describes a red-faced feeling: 'emb.............'?

O1  **Read the article. Then discuss in groups whether you think the results of a similar survey in your country would be the same.**

## Britain's teachers are as thick as the rest of us

In the first comprehensive survey of their ignorance, Britain's teachers have emerged as incapable of giving reliable answers to those odd little questions that sometimes pop into children's heads. They also have trouble with English, and problems with simple maths.

These are the findings of a survey, carried out by Market and Opinion Research International (Mori) for the Sunday Times.

More than 300 teachers from secondary, middle and primary schools throughout Britain were given 16 simple questions on current affairs, geography, spelling, maths, science, history and literature. The results suggest that many teachers should spend their free periods detained in one another's classes.

"What is 15% of £10?" teachers were asked; 16% gave the wrong answer or did not know, including 13% of the 171 maths and science teachers in our sample. Five per cent of maths and science teachers thought the answer was more than £1.50, 3% decided it was less, and 5% were so foxed they had to give up.

"Appalling," said Peter Dawson, general secretary of the Professional Association of Teachers, when told the result this weekend.

Spelling caused even more trouble. Only one in four teachers could spell all three words in our test, "embarrass", "satellite" and "harassment". Thirteen per cent got every word wrong.

Ninety-five per cent, however, knew who Nelson Mandela was (the imprisoned National Congress leader); and all but five teachers could explain who Kenneth Baker is (the Education Secretary, their boss). One teacher, however, asserted that Baker was Home Secretary, one thought he was "a newsreader" and one a Channel 4 presenter.

Capital cities were another difficult area. One in five teachers did not know the capital of Poland (Warsaw), 27% did not realise that West Germany's capital is Bonn, and 47% had not absorbed the capital of Afghanistan (Kabul), despite its receiving some publicity in recent years. Only 42% got the three capitals right.

One in 24 teachers thinks Ian Paisley, the Northern Ireland politician, is a Catholic (another mistake). And 11% of teachers could not say how many millimetres there are in a metre (1,000). One in five teachers did not know that King John signed the Magna Carta. Six teachers thought it was William the Conqueror and three that it was Henry VIII.

"The results of this survey would be laughable if they were not so devastating," said Dawson. "If you were the parent of a child faced with a teacher who cannot spell any of these words, and who cannot tell you what 15% of 10 quid is, you would have every reason to suppose that education is a national disaster area."

Sunday Times 30 October 1988

O2    **Read the article again carefully and arrange the questions in order according to how many correct answers were given by the British teachers — question(s) about:**

a) percentages   b) Nelson Mandela   c) spelling
d) the capital of W. Germany   e) Poland   f) Afghanistan
g) Ian Paisley   h) Kenneth Baker   i) the Magna Carta   j) millimetres

O3    **The article, as you can imagine, made some teachers rather angry. Look at what one teacher wrote in a note to a colleague after reading it:**

> Saw the enclosed article in one of last week's Sundays. Made my blood boil, I can tell you. These surveys just take a few hundred people and then have the nerve to relate it to the whole of the profession. Bet some of their spelling isn't so hot! What's more, you'd be hard put to it to find a line in that particular newspaper without a spelling, punctuation or printing mistake. As for the maths, some of these researchers must be living in the Dark Ages. Haven't they ever heard of calculators? I'm not saying we're perfect, but I object to them labelling us all as 'thickos'!

O4    **The scribbled note is in a very colloquial style. Think of more formal ways of expressing the following expressions, using the prompts in brackets:**

1 made my blood boil (irritated/annoyed)   3 isn't so hot (far from)
2 have the nerve to (impertinent)   4 you'd be hard put to it (rare)

O5    **Later that evening this incensed teacher wanted to write a letter of protest to the newspaper defending teaching standards. Read the following notes (1 and 2), then write the letter for him/her.**

1 He/She wanted to:
   – question the validity of the survey (a sample of 300 etc.)
   – suggest that some of the sample were treating it as a joke
   – cast doubt on the usefulness of such general knowledge anyway
   – claim that teaching standards in his/her area were as high as ever
   – attack journalists (and others) for low standards of literacy

2 He/She considered using some of these opening phrases:

| | |
|---|---|
| I feel I should point out that ... | I must stress that ... |
| I would seriously doubt whether ... | I can hardly imagine that ... |
| You might be interested to know that ... | I cannot believe that ... |
| According to ... , whereas in actual fact ... | I feel very strongly that ... |
| We are led to believe that ... . However, in reality, ... | |
| You refer to ... , but what is more to the point is that ... | |

O6    **Having read part of the article (opposite), you would now like to see**

a) a copy of the actual questionnaire given to the teachers, and
b) a copy of the complete statistical results.

**Write a brief letter to the organisation that conducted the survey.**

*O7*  **Below are the opening paragraphs of articles about our changing world.**

   **1  Read them to get a general idea of what you think each full article would be about. (Don't worry for the moment about the gaps in the texts.)**

1  The scene: a man is returning home ... car after finishing at the office. It's 4 a.m. (yes, many office staff will be working shifts ... then), and his wife is still out at work. Feeling ... stress, the man picks ... his car phone and rings his computerised home to give it a list of instructions. ... the time he arrives half an hour later, parks his car under his house, and approaches the front door, his orders have been carried out ... the letter.

2  Most people associate science and technology with progress, progress to a cleaner, safer world. We look to science to ... diseases and to technology to ... the quality of our lives. Whilst most of the discoveries of the last 50 years have proved beneficial, one in particular has left us with an appalling problem: the atom bomb. For the first time in the history of mankind there exist weapons which can ... the world.

3  The ... and sometimes ... procedure of transporting prisoners to and from jails and courtrooms has led one US county in Florida to install the world's ... "judicial video conferencing system".

4  The changing ... of life into the 1990s and the ... of the computer in the home becoming as commonplace as the electric ... are likely to have a significant ... on house prices by 1992.

5  A machine which ... dictation; a computerised mouse that can ... its way through a complex maze in seconds; a chess computer that can ... experts; detailed electronic images created with paint, charcoal or airbrush effects; radar that can ... up to 200 missiles coming from any direction; a database that can ... a doctor diagnose illness; a robot that ... up fruit – are these examples of Artificial Intelligence (AI), or not?

6  When we are 11, we go ... bed before 'News at 10' and get ... well with our parents. ... 12, one ... three of us knows the taste of cigarettes. By 13, British teenagers are more likely to buy alcohol and tobacco than spend their money ... books. ... all ages, the nation's secondary pupils spend about as much time watching television as they do ... the classroom.

7  ... the 1950s, when America became rich, the three gods of American consumerism – the television, the car, the mall – have grown ... together, feeding ... each other. Goods are advertised ... television, then people drive off ... their cars to the mall and buy them.

8  Never has an industry ... such a rapid transformation as that ... by financial services over the last three years. The move to a share-owning society, the changes ... by the Financial Services Act and new pensions legislation have ... their mark, as it seems, overnight. Yet there are dangers in such speed of change.

   **2  There are at least three words missing from each of the paragraphs. In each paragraph the same *kind* of word is missing.**

      a)  Decide what kind of word is missing in each paragraph (e.g. nouns, adjectives, prepositions, etc.).
      b)  Try to find a suitable word to go into each of the gaps.

   **3  At the top of p. 41 are groups of the words which appeared in the original articles. Find out where they belong, then compare them with your choices.**

| **a** | **c** | **d** | **e** | **f** | **h** |
|---|---|---|---|---|---|
| destroy | impact | cuts | under | first | at |
| enhance | pattern | help | by | dangerous | on |
| cure | kettle | track | by | costly | in |
| | prospect | find | to | **g** | to |
| **b** | | takes | up | off | on |
| made | | beat | by | on | at |
| experienced | | | | since | in |
| undergone | | | | up | |
| achieved | | | | in | |

**4** Here are eight headlines which go with the opening paragraphs you have read. Which headlines match which paragraphs?

> **Too fast, too soon?**
>
> **SATELLITE SHOPLAND – Shopping Centres of the Future**
>
> **Tune in for your trial**
>
> **Young Britain is growing up in a most alarming way**
>
> **2010 – TIME TO GO HOME**
>
> **HOME IS WHERE THE WORK IS**
>
> **ANYTHING YOU CAN DO ... IT CAN DO BETTER**
>
> **THE COMMAND AND CONTROL OF NUCLEAR WEAPONS**

**5** What things do you think each article might go on to comment on? Which do you think you would find most/least interesting? Why? Try to write a second paragraph for two or three of them. See if your partner(s) can decide which articles you are continuing.

*08* **Dictionary work**

Words in English have a habit of having more than one meaning, and can often be more than one part of speech. Even with common words like *free, lot* and *fit*, you may sometimes need to use a dictionary. Rewrite these sentences without using the words underlined. You can change the whole sentence around if necessary, but remember – your rewritten version will probably be in a different style.

1  The cry "<u>Free</u> Nelson Mandela!" has been answered.      **free**
   'BITE' – the alcohol-<u>free</u> lager.
   <u>Free</u> can of oil with every 20 litres purchased.

2  That's your <u>lot</u> for tonight, folks!      **lot**
   Very few people are happy with their <u>lot</u>.
   And the next <u>lot</u> is a pair of early 18th-century silver candlesticks.
   You hear a <u>lot</u> less about workers' strikes than you used to.

3  I don't think he will <u>fit</u> into this team.      **fit**
   Your father will have a <u>fit</u> when he finds out.
   These jeans are a tight <u>fit</u>.    The answer could be 'on', but it doesn't <u>fit</u>.
   It was a meal <u>fit</u> for a king.    I haven't felt so <u>fit</u> for years.

*A1*  **In Section 2 of the ARELS exam, you have to respond to remarks made to you. Match the seven suitable starters to responses with their meanings on the right.**

1 That's quite all right.
2 Far from it.
3 I'd rather you didn't.
4 I'm afraid not.
5 I wouldn't be surprised.
6 It's up to you.
7 Rather you than me.

a It's your decision./You decide.
b I'm sorry [I can't etc.]
c That's OK. I accept your apology.
d I'm glad I'm not in your position.
e Please don't do that.
f I think [it] probably [will].
g Quite the contrary.

These can be followed up with a second sentence, as in these examples:

1 A Aren't you tired of learning English?
  B Far from it. I'm enjoying it now more than ever.

2 A Could you lend me five pounds until tomorrow?
  B I'm afraid not. I haven't got a penny on me.

Listen to the cassette and respond to the comments you hear in a similar way, using the phrases 1–7 above as starters.

*A2*  **Look at the story opposite for a minute, then do exercises A3-A8.**

*A3*  **Look at Picture 1. Think about past tenses you could use to start your story. Make these into sentences to begin the story:**

The Smith family / watch / a show on television one evening ...
The Smiths / just finish / their dinner one evening last week ...
They / look forward to watching / The Eurovision Song Contest for ages ...

**As the story progresses, go on mixing your tenses with these prompts.**

The programme / just start / when / set / explode
Johnny / who / send upstairs when TV blow up / come downstairs
After he / try / repair / 90 minutes, / Mr Smith / on the point / give up

*A4*  1 **Try to use a range of vocabulary. Look at picture 4. How many adjectives can you think of to describe Mr Smith's feeling or mood at this moment?**

  2 **Try not to use the same words over and over again. There is a danger of your using the words *repair* and *television* four or five times when telling this story. For example, instead of *repair*, you could use *mend, fix* or *put (it) right*; and in place of *television*, you could use *the TV* or *the set*.**
  **Suggest other words or phrases that you could use to avoid repeating the words *angry, parts (of the set), explode* and *try*.**

*A5*  **Here are some phrases which you might use in your story. Which pictures would you use them with? And what sentences would you make with them?**

| | | |
|---|---|---|
| in search of | on the point of giving up | in vain |
| pleased with [himself] | put them together again | all over the place |
| in a matter of minutes | to [his] surprise | all of a sudden |

A6 **One other thing to bear in mind is how effective reported speech can sound when you are telling a story like this. Report the remarks below, like this:**

'Go upstairs.' (tell)   Johnny's mother told him to go upstairs.
'I'll fix it for you.' (say)   Johnny said (that) he'd/he would fix it for them.

1 'Where's my tool bag?' (ask)
2 'This won't take long.' (assure)
3 'It's time for bed.' (remind)
4 'I'm totally confused.' (admit)

5 'I think I know what has to be done.' (say)
6 'We learn about things like this at school.' (explain)

A7 **Listen to someone telling the story of Johnny and the television. Then you do it.**

A8 **Then tell the story as if you were little Johnny. And tell the story once more, but this time tell it as if you were Mr Smith.**

43

# UNIT 7 Holidays and Travel

### WARM-UP

**Make a list of ten essential things that you would pack in your hand-luggage if you were going on a plane journey to the other side of the world. Compare your list with other students': can you prove yours is more sensible than theirs? Use expressions like this:**

But surely you'd need ... ;
If you didn't have ... and (something happened), you'd ... .
And I think you'd be better off with a/an ... than a/an ... .
And what would you do without a/an ... if ...

**Between you, see if you can compromise and find the ideal list of items.**

### A1

**Listen to these sentences spoken on tape. They will each be spoken twice. What different 'message' is conveyed each time.**

1 Would you like something to eat or drink?
2 We aren't stopping at Birmingham, are we?
3 Is that the price of a return flight to Paris?
4 That was charming, I must say.
5 The reservation is for Mrs J. Smith.
6 The best time to come would be in May or June.
7 They're arriving on Sunday.
8 It didn't rain the whole week.

### A2

**Often when we speak (or read aloud) we want to list some items. For example:**

> *For the salad we need lettuce, cucumber, tomatoes and some goat's cheese.*

**Our voice normally goes up at the end of each item until the last, when it comes down. Sometimes, the voice doesn't come back down because the list is endless:**

> *Italy is full of beautiful places: Rome, Venice, Florence, Naples ...*

**Listen to these sentences spoken on tape, then practise reading them yourself:**

1 You can go to London via Southampton, Salisbury or Winchester.
2 These prices are only valid for March, April and June.
3 You can choose between full board at a hotel, half board at a guest-house or self-catering apartments.
4 You can have your potatoes boiled, fried, baked, ...
5 Would you like to see the menu now or sit in the bar and have a drink first?
6 Red, white or rosé?
7 Do you want to go sightseeing, or visit a museum, or go to the beach, or ...?
8 Then you have to add insurance, airport taxes, transport to and from the airport, spending money, ... it's not cheap.

*A3*  **Listen to some people starting sentences about their holidays. Decide from their tone of voice whether the following statements are true or false.**

|  | True | False |
|---|---|---|
| 1 He didn't enjoy the holiday much. | ☐ | ☐ |
| 2 She probably enjoyed her holiday. | ☐ | ☐ |
| 3 It was easy to make contact with local people. | ☐ | ☐ |
| 4 Things were expensive. | ☐ | ☐ |
| 5 The resort was over-commercialised. | ☐ | ☐ |
| 6 They stayed there more than two weeks. | ☐ | ☐ |

*A4*  **Tag questions (*isn't it? have you? weren't they?* etc.) convey many different things. Our voice usually falls when we are stating or confirming something we are pretty sure about, or expressing an opinion:**

> *It's been a very mild winter, hasn't it?*

**Our voice usually rises when we aren't sure of our facts or react with surprise:**

> *Good Heavens! It's not as late as that, is it?!*

**Now read aloud these comments made by friends looking at holiday snaps and reminiscing. Discuss why your voice rose or fell at the end of each sentence.**

1 Surely we didn't go out looking like that, did we?
2 One thing's for sure: it was a lovely beach, wasn't it?
3 I can't remember now; it was about 200 drachmas to the pound, wasn't it?
4 I remember those boys: they're the ones we met in Athens, aren't they?
5 Her name was Sandrine or er Jeanine or Sabine, wasn't it?
6 It seems a long time ago now, doesn't it?

*A5*  **Listen to this short dialogue, then read and practise it in pairs:**

LIZ: Do they have pesos or pesetas in Spain? I can't remember.
TOM: Pesetas, I think. Or is that Portugal?
LIZ: No, they have escudos or es-something in Portugal, don't they?
TOM: Why?
LIZ: Well, it's just that it says here you can hire a car for 30,000 of them for a week.
TOM: Does it say how many there are to the pound?
LIZ: No.
TOM: That's very useful!
LIZ: But I think overall the holiday itself is not too bad. For under £200 you get your return flight, 14 nights' full board (including wine with all your meals), excursions, free evening entertainment and a free bottle of Spanish brandy. Not bad, is it?
TOM: Is that for high season or is it the out of season price?
LIZ: Oh, come on! You don't expect those prices in July and August, do you?!
TOM: I only asked.
LIZ: Oh, no! Oh, that's great!
TOM: What is?
LIZ: These prices only apply for 'groups of over 20, children under 11 or old-age pensioners'. Charming!

*01* **Read this humorous Travel Guide sent in to a magazine by a reader, then do the exercises below. It's about going on holiday to the fictitious country of Outlandia.**

---

JANE BROWNING
*of Ontario, Canada, has sent us her*

# "Ghengis Khan Travel Guide to Outlandia".

1) Do not arrive in Outland City without some Outlandish currency, a basic knowledge of Outlandian, a tame tour guide or the name of at least three hotels. (The first two may not exist.)

2) Make sure your suitcase contains detergent, bleach and rat poison; if possible carry these in hand luggage too, as other luggage rarely arrives at the same time and place as its owner.

3) Also have in your hand luggage spare underwear, shoes, make-up, toothbrush and, very importantly, iron tablets.

4) Resist all offers of Kasapó, the locally brewed hooch. The Outlandian for gin and tonic is 'acknig e nontic'.

5) Before you leave, enrol on a course in bargaining and holding your breath (essential when using Outlandish WCs).

6) Do not pull up at traffic lights with car windows open; women and their jewellery are easily parted.

7) Do not step off the kerb in Outland City's streets; on second thoughts, do not walk anywhere near the kerb.

8) People with bad hearts, legs or heads, claustrophobic tendencies or sensitive ears should not use Outlandish public transport.

9) Take insect repellent, Kaolin and Morphine, antibiotics and bandages.

10) Do not go to Outlandia.

---

**1 Answer these questions about the Guide. In many cases you might have to read between the lines to infer the answer.**

1 What is the biggest problem with Outlandish toilets?
2 What indications are there of poor sanitary conditions in hotels?
3 What is the connection between items 2 and 3 above?
4 What do you think the standard of driving is like in Outlandia? Why?
5 What impression do we get of Outlandish buses and trams?
6 What do we learn about shopping etiquette in Outlandia?
7 Why should morphine and bandages be packed?
8 What suggests there might be a diet problem?
9 What appears to happen sometimes at traffic lights in Outland City?

**2 Add another 30-40 words to complete this postcard that Jane wrote from Outlandia to a friend back home in Canada:**

> Got here finally. Eventually found a place to stay – not without difficulty, I can tell you. No one here seems to speak English! Am under constant attack from insects of every shape, size and colour.

**3 You have had a disastrous holiday yourself, or you have been on a trip to a place where things were 'a little difficult'. Write a similar humorous Guide to the one above for visitors going to the place you have been to. (150-200 words.)**

02    **Read this letter of appointment that you received a few weeks before taking up a job as a tour guide.**

---

Dear Mr Black,

We are pleased to offer you the position of tour guide on our forthcoming series of summer tours to Belmos. Your appointment will commence on Friday, 30th June and terminate on Sunday, 27th August. Your duties during your period of employment with Sunshine Tours will be as follows:

- Escorting groups of no more than 20 holidaymakers from Belmos Airport to their accommodation
- Supervising the welfare of guests during their stay
- Escorting guests on excursions in conjunction with the local Sunshine Tours representative and his or her assistant

While at the resort, you will be working in close co-operation with our local representative, who will have overall responsibility for the day-to-day running of operations. In the event of an emergency, you will be expected to contact Head Office for guidance on the most suitable course of action to be taken.

You will not normally be expected to work more than twelve hours in any one day, and one day in seven will be a rest day. Your basic pay will be £105 per week, to cover all duties carried out while in the service of Sunshine Tours. A record of expenses should be kept throughout your period of employment; these will be reviewed at the end of your contract.

We would ask you to sign the copy of this letter that we are enclosing as confirmation of acceptance of our offer and return it to us without delay.

We look forward very much to your joining our staff at the end of this month.

Yours sincerely,

---

**During your period of employment a number of things went wrong. Here are a few notes from the diary that you kept. Read them, then do the exercise overpage:**

> 35 people on this holiday. 29 on the last one. What was all that about 20 maximum? Finding accommodation for the extra numbers virtually impossible. Lots of disgruntled people.
>
> No sign of the local rep. Am having to handle everything alone. Am absolutely shattered! It's basically an 18-hour day and the idea of a day off is a joke!
>
> Accident on the boat-trip today. Phoned through to Head Office — no help or guidance whatsoever. They just didn't want to know. Just hope that the travel insurance Mrs Jackson has got is going to cover her.

**When you finish your contract, you write a letter (about 300 words) to the company that employed you, suggesting that, in the light of the conditions under which you were working, they might review the wages that were paid to you.**

**Point out the inaccuracies in the job specification that was sent to you and describe the reality of your situation. You might use language such as this:**

| | |
|---|---|
| I was led to believe that ... | In actual fact, ... |
| According to my letter of appointment, ... | As things turned out, ... |
| I was assured/informed/promised/told that ... | |
| Imagine my surprise/disappointment/dismay/annoyance when ... | |

O3   **You were not the only one who was dissatisfied with Sunshine Tours. Mrs Jackson nearly drowned during her 'unforgettable fortnight in paradise'! This is the brochure she read before she booked her holiday.**

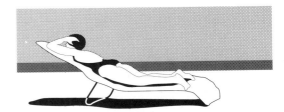

This could be you, basking in fourteen hours of sunshine every day, going on unforgettable trips of exploration in scenery you've probably only ever dreamed of. Isn't it time you let yourself be spoilt?
Don't you deserve it?

Let us spoil you.
We have years of experience of island holidays and our experienced staff are always on hand to make this a holiday you'll never forget. For the whole of the fortnight you won't have to lift a finger.

From the moment you arrive at Gatwick Airport to the moment you return, we'll cater for your every whim.

Enjoy a full programme of conducted tours and supervised activities, where everything has been organised for you, right down to the minutest detail.

The cost of your holiday includes

- flights to and from Belmos Airport with airport transfer to hotel
- daily trips by coach, minibus or romantic horse and carriage to other parts of this paradise island and boat trips to neighbouring islands
- the round-the-clock services of our expert team of guides
- fully-comprehensive personal insurance in the event of accident

- full board accommodation in the island's most luxurious hotel

There are no hidden extras and no surcharges; that's guaranteed!

**And this is the letter she wrote to you, Mark, the guide, from her hospital bed on Belmos.**

Dear Mark,

Thank you very much for your kind note. I'm as well as can be expected; the torn ligaments are healing reasonably well and the doctor says the lung problem is just a matter of wait and see.

Please don't blame yourself for what happened. That boat must have been a contemporary of the Ark – rotten through and through. The rail gave way at the slightest touch. It really was the last straw. The organisation has been a joke, the hotel a disgrace and the promised schedule, as you know all too well, a complete non-event.

When I write to Sunshine – as of course I will – I'll stress that you were doing all you could in impossible circumstances. They have got a lot to answer for. What they write in their brochure is so far removed from the truth a good lawyer would have a field day. I shall tell them in very strong terms about the shortage of accommodation, the cancellation of just about every scheduled excursion, the delays, the lack of information etc. As for their attitude so far to the question of my compensation, it's incredible that I've heard nothing yet. I shall have to insist that they pay in full; hospital charges here are not cheap, as you know.

Anyway, enough of my worries. Thank you again for your concern. Perhaps we'll meet again some time in happier circumstances.

Yours sincerely,

Celia Jackson

04   **Write Mrs Jackson's letter to Sunshine Tours, explaining what happened, criticising the general running of the holiday and asking for compensation for her accident. Consider including phrases such as these in the letter:**

| | |
|---|---|
| In the first place, ... | As if this were not enough, ... |
| In addition to this, ... | To make matters even worse,... (And) to cap it all, ... |

| | | |
|---|---|---|
| In the light of all this, | } { | I am sure you would wish to ... |
| Considering what has happened, | | could I suggest that you ... |

# UNIT 8 This Working Life

## WARM-UP

**What do you want from a job? What are (or will be) the most important criteria for you personally in a job or career? Order the points below 1-10 (where 1 = the most important for you): then justify your order to a partner, a group or the class.**

- Variety of tasks
- Responsibility for others or for decisions
- Wages/Salary
- Pleasant surroundings, understanding boss, pleasant people to work with
- Extras or 'perks' such as a clothes/uniform allowance, a car, etc.

- Opportunity for promotion
- Training and/or apprenticeship scheme
- Security (e.g. a 5-year contract)
- Flexible working hours
- Paid holidays

## O1   Dictionary work

**1 Opposite is a letter of application for a job. In order to try to make a good impression, John has typed it instead of writing it by hand. Unfortunately, however, he has made quite a few spelling mistakes.**
**Read the letter carefully, circle the words he has misspelt and correct them. Use your dictionary if you need to. Check your findings with a partner.**

**2 Using your English-English dictionary, find other words or expressions to replace these from the letter. Would the replacements change the style of the letter at all?**

1 position;   2 issue;   3 at present;   4 took;   5 confident;
6 attached;   7 match;   8 outlined

## O2   Put yourself in Mrs Bracknell's position. She is quite impressed by the tone of the letter (and by John's qualifications and experience given in his CV) – but not by his spelling. However, in the job he's applied for, good spelling is not absolutely essential, so she'd like him to come for an interview. In about 200 words, write the letter for her. Reorganise and use these ideas:

- Pleased J took a job for experience, rather than go on the dole – shows character
- Suggest he obtain a letter of reference from the Leisure Centre manager
- Come for interview – suggest date and time
- Stress he must be able to drive
- Express concern about his spelling – suggest he go on a course
- Thank J for his application
- Brief outline of trainee scheme: 3-month probation period – under guidance of senior salesman. Further 6 months' training + day-release course in marketing at local college.

                                                  180, High Street,
                                                        Longfield,
                                                      Middletown,
                                                      Greenshire

Mrs M. Bracknell,
Personel Officer,
Smith & Smith Ltd.,
Unit 25, Gloucester Rd.,
Hightown Industriel Estate,
Hightown                                          28th March, 1990



Dear Mrs Bracknell,

I write with referance to the position of trainee
saleman which you advertised in yesterday's issue of
"Job World" magasine.

At present I am employed on the Reception Desk at the
Hightown Leasure Centre, a job which I took more for
exsperience than as a career prospecte when I left
college earlyer this year. However, I would very much
like to go into sales, and I feel confident you will
find (in the attached CV) that my qualifecations match
those outlined in your advertisment.

Since my working hours at the Centre are fairly
flexable, I could attend for interview at almost any
time conveniant to you.

I look foreward to hearing from you.

Yours faithfully,

*John Street*

John Street

encl. CV and examination diplomas.

*03*  Not everyone works (or even wants to work) for someone else.
The following exercises refer to the article opposite which appeared in *The Times* newspaper on Friday, 9th October, 1987.

1  Before you read the article, use your English-English dictionary to look up the word 'chatelaine' (quite rare in English!) and explain the headline.

From the section title *Your Own Business*, the headline, and the photo and caption, what do you think the article might be about?

2  Read the first five paragraphs of the article carefully (from the beginning down to '... are near Stroud.').  Using only the information contained in those paragraphs, say whether these statements are *true* or *false* – and give reasons.

a)  Ms Roach sells keys to cottage-owners.
b)  She looks after cottages that belong to older residents.
c)  The cottage owners don't live in them permanently.
d)  More and more people are coming to live and work in Gloucestershire.
e)  Three royal couples live in the area where Ms Roach has set up business.

3  Now read the rest of the article (from 'Ms Roach saw a market ...') and write down *ten questions* that you think the journalist Brian Collett asked Harriet Roach in order to write his article. Here are three examples:

a)  When did you form or start Cottage Concern?
b)  Did you start the business on your own, or with someone else?
c)  What (kind of) service do you offer your clients?

4  Now work with another student and compare the questions you each wrote. Correct each other's English (if necessary!) and decide whether your questions would have elicited all the information needed for the article.

*04*  You were very impressed with the idea and success of Cottage Concern. You think you would like to write a more detailed article (for an English-language magazine in your own country) about how Ms Roach organises her work and her family life, or about how she managed to get started.

Write her a letter, with a tentative approach, in about 200 words. Use some of these questions and notes as a guide:

– Will this be a formal or an informal letter? So will you really need her address? Can you find it in the article? If not, why not write to her c/o *The Times* newspaper? (If you do this, what two words would you write on the envelope to show that you want the letter sent on to Ms Roach?)
– Refer to the article – express interest in the idea of 'Cottage Concern'.
– Explain why you're interested in writing your article.
– Ask a number of questions which indicate the kind of points you're interested in: these should lead to full answers for your article.
– Ask permission to telephone her some time to ask these and other questions, and enquire when might be a convenient time to call.
– How will you close your letter?

## YOUR OWN BUSINESS

# The cottage chatelaine

**By Brian Collett**

A young mother dashing around the countryside with a collection of house keys hardly seems a symbol of social change. Harriet Roach considers she performs a useful service to the owners of West Country cottages but in reality her new business reflects Britain's new-found prosperity.

Ms Roach runs Cottage Concern, keeping a watch over town-dwellers' holiday homes in rural Gloucestershire, when they are unoccupied.

From her own cottage in Bisley, between Stroud and Cirencester, Ms Roach had noticed more cottages being bought by people from outside Gloucestershire for holidays and week-end breaks.

"Gloucestershire has always been fashionable," she says. "It's also becoming a bit yuppie now, to be honest. I think perhaps it has become even more popular in the past five to seven years, since the royals moved in."

The Prince and Princess of Wales are at Highgrove, near Tetbury, the Princess Royal and Captain Mark Phillips at Gatcombe Park, near Minchinhampton, and Prince and Princess Michael of Kent are near Stroud.

Ms Roach saw a market to be tapped in the new social trend and formed Cottage Concern in June last year, with her neighbour Elspeth Williams as her partner to cover in her absence.

"Really we give a caretaker service without living in," she explains. "We carry out security checks, we see that all appliances are working, and we organize any maintenance that has to be done.

"We tidy up after the people have gone, though we stress that we are not a cleaning service. We arrange for cleaners if they are needed. We do cooking and put the food in the freezer.

"In the bad weather we see that there

**Harriet Roach: Taking the strain on the chores**

are no leaking pipes, and if there is trouble we sort it out. If a burglar alarm rings in the middle of the night we go out and switch the thing off!

"We believe that if you work hard to afford your country cottage you shouldn't have to spend time doing the chores."

There are also many property-owners in this affluent area who leave their homes for long spells, either for business trips or to pass the winter in a warmer climate — another sign of a changing social pattern.

Ms Roach recalls: "Last winter the heating packed up at a very big house while the owners were in the States. The radiators began leaking and water was dripping down the walls. We sorted it out, and the owners were very pleased when they came back."

Cottage Concern charges customers £40-£50 a month for one visit a week, and £5 an hour for extra services. After a quiet start to the year Ms Roach has six customers on the books, finding that business is generated by word of mouth rather than media advertising.

Although the service offered by Cottage Concern looks like part of a growing trend, Ms Roach says: "I don't know of anybody else in this line. There's certainly nobody else in this area."

There was another reason why she set up Cottage Concern. "Having four children at school, I couldn't do a 9 to 5 job," she says. "Employers, especially in this area, are short-sighted about women who can't be there all the time. I'm surprised there are not more people working on flexi-hours."

*A1*   **In the ARELS exam you may be asked to take part in a short telephone conversation while you look at a note, an advertisement, a plan of a house, a person's business card, etc. In the exam you would normally have less to read than in this practice activity.**

Susan, a friend of yours, left a magazine called ***Mod Media*** at your house or apartment when she dropped in to see you yesterday. She telephones and asks you to give her the information contained in an advertisement which she has circled in the 'SITS VACANT' column on page 19 of the magazine.

**First, study the ad and answer the questions below:**

**19 • M O D   M E D I A**

**Situations vacant**

## Secretary / PA to Director
# Pro-graphics

We are a small but growing company in the field of design and graphics. As we are expanding, we now require an experienced Secretary / Personal Assistant for the Director of our Advertising and Promotions Dept.

Duties for the successful applicant will include all those expected of a Secretary in a busy office PLUS working closely with the Director on advertising and promotions. Some experience in advertising and graphic design would therefore be useful. Typing and word processing experience are essential. We shall be looking for someone who can use his or her initiative and who can work under pressure.

**Salary: £10,000–£12,000 negotiable**
Includes 6 weeks' paid holiday and company pension scheme.

Apply to **Personnel Officer, Pro-Graphics, St Stephen's House, Leicester Ave., Hightown.** ☎ **Hightown 123321**

1  What job is the company advertising?
2  What's the name of the company?
3  Must the successful applicant be experienced?
4  What wages or salary are they offering?
5  What will the job entail?
6  What other extras or 'perks' are offered?
7  Who must applicants write to? Can you spell out the name and address?
8  Is a phone number given? Could you read it out?

*A2*  Now look at the advertisement, listen and take part in the conversation. Remember,
[cassette]  the information given in the situation and in the ad should guide what you say.

*A3*  Giving a short persuasive talk on a prepared topic

Here is a selection of topics related to the theme of 'this working life'. Read them
carefully, choose one, write brief notes, then be prepared to give a two-minute talk
on your topic to a small group or the class.
IMPORTANT: You should refer back to the guidance in Unit 4, pages 30-31.

**Topics**

1 I'm just the person you need to set up a company selling British products in
  my country.

2 Unemployment makes people ill.

3 My ideal job.

4 The ideal is to make money out of your favourite pastime.

5 In this day and age it's better to have a job you don't really enjoy than to
  have no job at all.

*A4*  Oral grammar exercises in the ARELS exam are usually connected with a picture
story. This exercise is connected with the topic of work in general.
You work in a small firm and are present at the Annual General Meeting. Here are
some of the things people say. Express the sentences in a different way beginning
with the words given in brackets.

Example:  We should have spent more on advertising last year. (I wish ...)
          *I wish we'd/we had spent more on advertising last year.*

1 It's a long time since our profits were so low.  (We haven't ...)
2 I think we should have no salary rises this year.  (I suggest ...)
3 We got into trouble because the bank manager wasn't helpful.  (If the bank
  manager ...)
4 I'd prefer us not to take a vote on the proposal just yet.  (I'd rather ...)
5 We took on ten new machine operators last year.  (Ten new machine
  operators ...)
6 Production needs to be increased by at least 20% next year.  (We need ...)

[cassette]  Now listen to the cassette and do more items like this.

# UNIT 9 Spaceship Earth

## WARM-UP AND DICTIONARY WORK

**Discuss these questions in pairs or groups, and use an English-English dictionary whenever necessary:**

**1 Why do we now talk about 'Spaceship Earth'? What has Earth got in common with a spaceship?**

**2 Some manufacturers in Britain have recently begun to put stickers like these on aerosol spray cans which contain such things as hair lacquer, deodorant, air freshener, spray furniture polish and so on.**

Note: CFC = chlorofluorocarbon.
CFCs are a group of chemicals used in the manufacture of some aerosols, plastic foam and refrigerator equipment; it is now generally accepted that they are having a serious effect on the earth's atmosphere.

1 Can you explain the phrase 'ozone friendly'?
2 Are manufacturers in your country doing anything about the CFC situation? If so, what? If not, do you think they should?
3 Can you suggest alternatives to using aerosol sprays?
4 What can be done about other forms of pollution such as industrial effluent and exhaust fumes from motor vehicles?

*A1* **You are going to hear an interview with Allan Thornton, Chairman of the Environmental Investigation Agency, talking about an endangered species.**

**1 Listen to the interview once to find answers to these questions:**

1 Which endangered species is Allan talking about?
2 Which different countries are mentioned in connection with the illegal trade?

**2 Now listen to the second part of the interview again and try to answer the questions on the cassette.**

**3 Now listen to another part of the same interview and fill in this table.**

| Year(s) | 1950s | 1979 | 1981 | 1986 | Present |
|---|---|---|---|---|---|
| Estimated numbers | | | | | |

**4 Discuss your reactions to the figures and their implications with a partner, then with the rest of the class. What do you think can or should be done about the situation?**

*A2*    One of the sections in the ARELS exam tests your responses to remarks made by other people. You might, for example, want a) to sympathise or commiserate, or b) to criticise or comment on other people's actions – and you can often do that with a short exclamation. Here are just a few. Study them and say which you would use to sympathise or commiserate, and which to criticise or comment.

| | |
|---|---|
| How marvellous/awful/annoying! | (Oh,) what a shame! |
| That's marvellous/awful/annoying! | (Oh,) what a pity! |
| How embarrassing!/ I bet that was embarrassing! | (Oh,) what a nuisance! |
| | What a (nice) surprise! |
| That must have terrible/annoying/ embarrassing! | That must have been a shock/ quite a surprise! |
| What a (terrible/stupid) thing to say! | What a way to behave! |
| What a (stupid/silly) thing to do! | What a question! |

**Now use the exclamations above as appropriate to respond to these remarks:**

1 'Do you know, a lot of people on the camp site were just throwing their rubbish in a stream behind the caravans.'
2 'When I last saw John, he said he thought the whole business of endangered species was a load of rubbish.'
3 'I can't come to the meeting, I'm afraid. I've got a Keep Fit class that evening.'
4 'They've just set up a Wildlife Protection Club in our area.'
5 'The local council have just sold half the forest land near us to be redeveloped for housing.'

*A3*    Now listen to the cassette and respond to more remarks in the same way.

*A4*    You have already practised responding to situations in Units 1 and 5 (pages 9 and 32). Look back briefly at those pages again. Here are some more situations: they all have some connection with our theme of 'Spaceship Earth'. Read each, then suggest two or three different ways to respond appropriately.

1 You go into a supermarket to buy some spray polish, hair lacquer and deodorant, but can find none with an *Ozone Friendly* label. What do you say when you find an assistant or the manager?
2 Someone invites you to dinner next Saturday and then says: 'By the way, is there anything you don't eat? I was thinking of cooking veal.' What do you say?
3 You're out on a picnic with some friends and you see one of them drop a chocolate bar wrapper. There's a rubbish bin nearby. What do you say to him or her?
4 A member of Greenpeace, the Friends of the Earth or some other group concerned with world ecology asks if you will put a poster advertising their cause in the window of your apartment or your car. What do you say?
5 Someone stops you in the street and asks for a contribution towards the upkeep of a local zoo. You refuse, but politely. What do you say?

*A5*    Now listen to the cassette and respond to more similar situations.

O1   In March 1989 the *Radio Times* magazine in Britain published a questionnaire entitled 'How green are you?'. It was part of a survey designed to find out what people are doing (or would do) to help the environment.

1   'Green' is a colour; it can also mean 'inexperienced, innocent'. But can you explain what it means in the title 'How green are you?'?

2   Here are questions 6 and 10 from the questionnaire. Read them and do as instructed. (Use a dictionary where necessary.) Then compare and discuss your answers with other students'.

---

### WILDLIFE AND COUNTRYSIDE

**Q.6** Please indicate how you feel, about the effects of each of the following on wildlife and the countryside.
Tick the far right hand box if you feel you don't know enough about it.

How worried?

| | Very | Quite | Not very | Not at all | Don't know enough |
|---|---|---|---|---|---|
| New roads | 1 | 2 | 3 | 4 | 5 |
| Industrial development | 1 | 2 | 3 | 4 | 5 |
| Natural disasters | 1 | 2 | 3 | 4 | 5 |
| Farm pollution | 1 | 2 | 3 | 4 | 5 |
| Bloodsports | 1 | 2 | 3 | 4 | 5 |
| Neglect of unmanaged areas of farmland | 1 | 2 | 3 | 4 | 5 |
| Dumping waste | 1 | 2 | 3 | 4 | 5 |
| New housing | 1 | 2 | 3 | 4 | 5 |
| Commercial forestry | 1 | 2 | 3 | 4 | 5 |

### PACKAGING AND WASTE

**Q.10** Here is a list of ways in which you can help reduce waste. Please indicate by ticking the appropriate box your own position regarding each of these courses of action. If you feel you do not know enough about some of these problems, you can place a tick in the far right hand column.

| | I do already | I'd seriously consider | I might consider | I'd never consider | Don't know enough |
|---|---|---|---|---|---|
| Take glass to the bottle bank | 1 | 2 | 3 | 4 | 5 |
| Compost kitchen waste | 1 | 2 | 3 | 4 | 5 |
| Re-use plastic carrier bags | 1 | 2 | 3 | 4 | 5 |
| Use recycled paper | 1 | 2 | 3 | 4 | 5 |
| Write on both sides of notepaper | 1 | 2 | 3 | 4 | 5 |
| Re-use envelopes | 1 | 2 | 3 | 4 | 5 |
| Buy fruit and vegetables loose rather than pre-packed | 1 | 2 | 3 | 4 | 5 |
| Send old clothes to an Oxfam shop/jumble sale | 1 | 2 | 3 | 4 | 5 |
| Buy the biggest size packet of washing powder, cornflakes, etc | 1 | 2 | 3 | 4 | 5 |

---

*O2*  **Using the questions (and your answers) opposite as a springboard, discuss, plan and write the following with a partner:**

1  A letter (about 200 words) to an English newspaper or magazine in your country urging people to take action on the problem of packaging and waste.
2  A persuasive letter to a friend (about 200 words), whom you know to be rather wasteful, urging him/her to consider changing his/her habits.

**NOTE:**
**The following exercises O3-O6 are based on the article reproduced on pages 60-61.**

*O3*  1  **Look at the headline, the subtitle and the map and its caption. How much do they tell you of what the article will be about?**
      2  **Now read the article quickly. Did it say what you thought it would say?**

*O4*  **Read the article more carefully and use the information to answer the following questions. Where you are asked to say whether a statement is True or False, give reasons. Discuss your answers with a partner and the class.**

1  Why is the British reader asked to 'picture [himself] in a job that begins at 10am and ends at 7pm'?
2  The amount of $CO_2$ in the atmosphere has always been on the increase. True or False?
3  Why, according to the writer, is there 'an irreversible warming of the planet'?
4  It has been forecast that the world's mean temperature could rise between 2°C and 5.2°C. What general effect would that have on Britain's climate?
5  Why might there be fewer deaths from heart attacks?
6  Why might there be fewer deaths too from other causes?
7  If the earth's temperature rose, there would be a steady decline in the death rate. True or False?
8  What would be the worst effect of a 5°C global rise in temperature?
9  The article seems to suggest that 50% of the population of Great Britain lives near the sea. True or False?
10  What would the effect of massive flooding in Britain be on agriculture?
11  What effects could such a change in climate have on a) our trees, b) the food we buy, c) wildlife?
12  The answer to the problem is to adopt nuclear energy 100%. True or False?

*O5*  **Use a dictionary to explain to a partner the following words and phrases as used in the article. We have indicated which column you will find them in.**

1  'tracts (of land)' (col. 1)          5  'a flip side' (col. 6)
2  'picture yourself' (col. 1)          6  'render ... untenable' (col. 7)
3  'compiled' (col. 2)                  7  'their mainstay' (col. 8)
4  'mean temperature' (col. 3)          8  'a shorter shelf life' (col. 8)

*O6*  **What do you think the effects might be on your own country of a global rise in temperature of something like 4°-5°C? Write an article (of about 300 words) for an English magazine, giving it an eye-catching headline and outlining some of the more important effects as you see them. Try to use some of the language you have read in the article.**

## WEEK IN REVIEW: BRITAIN

# Will a sunnier Britain

● Extremes of heat, swarms of insects, tracts of land under water: the greenhouse effect could transform the country by 2050, writes AMIT ROY

IMAGINE staying in Britain during the summer, basking in much drier, sunnier conditions, and enjoying a more relaxed, sociable Mediterranean-style of café culture.

Picture yourself in a job that begins at 10am and ends at 7pm, broken by a two-and-a-half hour siesta.

Think about what life would be like if there was a rapid decline in the country's birthrate, and fewer people died from heart disease.

Then visualise the sea washing through the streets of Canvey Island, Bristol, Avonmouth, Cardiff, Hull, Portsmouth, Morecambe, Great Yarmouth, Lowestoft and Felixstowe.

In the next 50 to 100 years these are just some of the potential consequences of the "greenhouse effect". This has been caused by a mounting concentration in the atmosphere of carbon dioxide ($CO_2$) created by burning fossil fuels such as coal, oil and natural gas, and it is leading to an irreversible warming of the planet because the $CO_2$ acts as a heat trap.

The Department of the Environment, which is al-

GREENHOUSE: How the changing weather will alter Britain

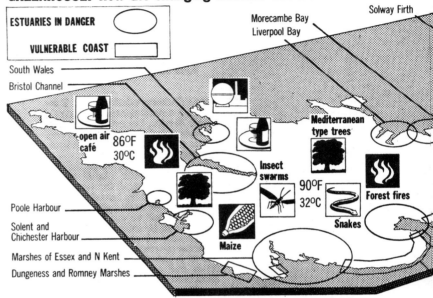

| ESTUARIES IN DANGER | |
| VULNERABLE COAST | |

Solway Firth
Morecambe Bay
Liverpool Bay
South Wales
Bristol Channel
open air café 86°F 30°C
Mediterranean type trees
Insect swarms
90°F 32°C
Forest fires
Poole Harbour
Solent and Chichester Harbour
Maize
Snakes
Marshes of Essex and N Kent
Dungeness and Romney Marshes

Hotter climes mean open-air cafés, new crops and trees, snakes, insect swarms, and vineyard

ready spending millions on researching the effects of global warming, last week allocated a further £250,000 for research. Earlier this year it published a report on the Possible Impacts of Climate Change on the Natural Environment in the United Kingdom, compiled from the work of six groups of scientists.

This and other research, being carried out by geographers and scientists at universities throughout Britain, indicates that the effects will touch nearly every aspect of our lives.

A recent study by Sir John Mason, director-general of the Meteorological Office for 18 years until 1983, said the world's mean temperature would rise between 2C and 5.2C if the $CO_2$ output was not checked.

This means that by the year 2050, a typical summer's day in southern Britain could have a temperature of 32C. There may be longer, drier and sunnier spells in the south, while northern areas and Scotland although warmer, may well a lot wetter.

The type of society would develop — with fe British men growing beard wearing ties — is describe Dr Nicholas Middleton of ford University.

For example, the birth-will fall because the hotter temperature the lower male's sperm count and female's fertility. "Interco is also less frequent in weather," says Middleton

## THE SUNDAY TIMES 13 NOVEMBER 1988

# varm to the café culture?

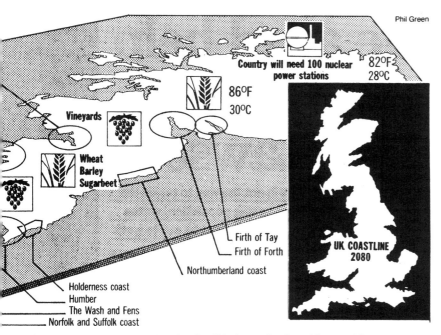

Phil Green

Country will need 100 nuclear power stations

82°F
28°C

86°F
30°C

Vineyards

Wheat
Barley
Sugarbeet

Firth of Tay
Firth of Forth
Northumberland coast

UK COASTLINE 2080

Holderness coast
Humber
The Wash and Fens
Norfolk and Suffolk coast

**north, but forecasts also suggest burning fossil fuels may lead to widespread flooding (inset)**

n Britain, maximum ception occurs in months h an average temperature ween 14C and 16C, while minimum is at a temature of 23C, when the rm count is low.

s we would eat less — nimum daily calorie conption in Britain is 2,520 in warmer Portugal it is y 2,450 — there would be er deaths from heart atks. At present 292 per ,000 people in Britain die m coronary problems,

compared with as few as 50 in Spain. Death-rates from cerebro-vascular and from respiratory and other breathing diseases are also likely to decline. One study shows that in London for every 1C rise in temperature, the mortality rate would drop by 2.5%. For 5C, the drop would be 12.5%.

However, there is a flip side to the story. Middleton believes that the climatic changes could mean extreme events becoming more frequent. "In a heatwave, the

death rate would rise markedly. The lowest socio-economic groups confined to cities would suffer most."

David Everest, formerly chief scientific officer for environmental pollution at the Department of the Environment, says the worst effect of a 5C rise in global tememperature would be flooding. The sea could rise by more than 1.5 metres. Indeed he believes that if ice breaks off in the Antarctic and falls into the sea — like ice cubes into a full glass — it could cause "surges", raising the water by as much as 5 metres. This would cover huge areas of Britain *(see map)* and force perhaps half the 56m population to move inland.

The effects on remaining agriculture could also be catastrophic. The drier soil in the south would probably render wheat, barley, sugar beet and potato cultivation untenable. These crops would have to be

moved north, while southern farmers would be forced to adopt crops such as maize (sweetcorn) as their mainstay.

The look of Britain's landscape would also be radically altered by changes in forestry. Spruce and conifers, the main British trees, could be replaced by species such as sweet chestnut (now confined to Kent), red and turkey oak, red alder, box tree, field maple, South America's southern beech and broad-leaved lime.

The rising temperature could lead to people becoming more irritable. There could be an increase in food poisoning. Bread, cakes and fresh pro-·duce would have a shorter shelf life. Insect swarms could invade Britain, and snakes would become more abundant.

Scientists believe the worst effects could be moderated by energy conservation and international agreements to cut down $CO_2$ and other greenhouse gases such as methane, nitrous oxide, ozone and chlorofluorocarbons.

And nuclear power is seen by Margaret Thatcher and Nicholas Ridley, her environment secretary, as the obvious way to reduce emission of $CO_2$. But in 50 years, allowing for more efficient plants and increasing demand for electricity, nearly 100 nuclear power stations would be needed.

The flooding threat could be countered by rebuilding Britain's coastal defences and redesigning the Thames barrier. But this would cost £5 billion at today's prices.

"We may be further ahead in the greenhouse effect that we have realised," Everest says. "Even if we stopped burning fossil fuels, the temperature would continue to rise because the build-up of carbon dioxide has taken place. The temperature has risen 0.5C since 1900 and it is accelerating."

# <sup>UNIT</sup>10  You and Your Food

_WARM-UP AND DICTIONARY WORK_

1  a  **Write down these four headings, and in two minutes list as many meats, vegetables, fruits and dairy products as you can. Then check your lists with other students'.**

**Meat        Vegetables        Fruit        Dairy products**

b  **Working with a partner, and using a dictionary, write down (in 2 minutes) as many ways as you can think of to prepare and cook some of the foods you have listed in a.**

2  **Write down your average diet for a week. Note what you have for breakfast, lunch and evening meal. Note what kinds of drinks you have, and what snacks you eat between meals. Discuss your diet with two or three partners: Do you have too much of one thing? Do you have too little? etc.**

_O1_  **Opposite is the beginning of an article that appeared in the *Sunday Express Magazine* in February 1989. Read the first five paragraphs carefully (from the beginning to '... fish or lean meat.'), and find a suitable word for each blank.**

_O2_  **Explain to a partner the following words and phrases as used in the article. We have indicated which paragraph you will find them in.**

1  a meat-and-two-veg race (para. 7)      4  toxicity (para. 9)
2  demi-vegetarianism (para. 7)           5  side-effects (para. 9)
3  chain of events (para. 9)

_O3_  **Here are some definitions from an English-English dictionary. Read them carefully and find the words or phrases in the text opposite that they define.**

1  (adj) too much; (para.6)
2  unpleasant; not wanted (para.6)
3  the belief in and practice of eating only fruit, vegetables, nuts, etc., or of avoiding eating meat and fish, usu. for reasons of health or religion (para.7)
4  increasing (para.7)
5  of living  things or the substances related to them (para.8)
6  a general direction or course of development; tendency (para.8)
7  to gather (a crop) (para.8)

_O4_  **Many articles like this have frequent section headings. Read the article again and suggest headings (or titles) for these pairs or groups of paragraphs:**

Paras. 1 and 2;  Paras. 3 and 4;  Paras. 5 and 6;  Paras. 7, 8 and 9;  Paras. 10 and 11

# FOOD FOR LIFE

## Sunday Express Magazine's comprehensive guide to healthy eating

Food gives you life and can keep you fit, but it may also make you fat and, like anything taken to   **1**  , can kill you. The Royal Society of Medicine tells us that 180,000 people a year in this country  **2**  of coronary heart disease, yet, caught in time, some of these deaths are   **3**   through exercise and, most importantly, through improved diet.

The World Health Organisation estimates that 35 per cent of cancers are also   **4**   with diet. "Excess fat intake has been linked to an increased incidence of cancers of the breast and colon, while food preservation techniques (for   **5**  , adding salt) have been associated with stomach cancer."

Latest figures show that one in four of us will be   **6**   by cancer at some point, and one in five will die from it. And,   **7**   with smoking and alcoholism, obesity is also a   **8**   factor. Yet more than 75 per cent of cancers are now   **9**   preventable through better diet and health education.

It is now quite clear to scientists and doctors that **10** many animal fats cause "elevated serum cholesterol" which, in **11** , is one of the main **12** of heart attacks. The fat furs up the arteries, which then pack up.

The World Health Organisation lays down **13** for healthy nutrition. These include eating less animal fat in all its forms, from butter (½lb is equivalent in dairy fats to 3½ pints of milk) through processed foods, to meat itself. Each day we should try to eat meals that contain a   **14**   of carbohydrates from fruits, vegetables and wholegrain cereals,

and protein from beans and pulses, as **15** as from low-fat dairy products, fish or lean meat.

Salt and sugar should be eaten far less than they are. The human body needs no extra salt – other than that occurring naturally in a well-balanced wholefood diet. Excessive salt contributes to hypertension and strokes. Sugar is bad for your teeth and, like anything else in excess, is transformed into undesirable fat.

People are becoming aware of these points; they want to know more, eat better, get back to nature. Major changes are taking place. No longer a meat-and-two-veg race, many households in Britain today are likely to be sitting down to three veg and no meat. Vegetarianism and demi-vegetarianism (which includes fish and white meat) are both on the increase.

Using food as a focus, we can examine the trend towards more natural ways of living. We can look at diet and nutrition in the context of how we harvest and prepare our food.

There is a natural chain of events that links the soil, animals, plants, the seasons and our food. Chemically-impregnated soil and hormone-injected animals lead to some degree of toxicity in food, the side-effects of which in humans are only now being recognised.

The food revolution in Britain has come in the shape of healthfoods, wholefoods, organic products and vegetarianism.

To clarify: healthfoods are associated with vitamins and supplements; wholefoods are unrefined and unprocessed; organic produce is grown in chemical-free soil; and vegetarianism is a diet from which meat and fish are excluded.

O5  Take-away food is quite popular in Britain. In June 1987 *Self Health*, a British magazine, conducted a survey on take-away meals. They bought one portion each of 14 meals and weighed and assessed them for their nutrition content.

The average British diet contains too much fat and too little fibre, and some take-aways (e.g. fish and chips) combine a high fat content with a low fibre count. But there's no harm in eating a take-away meal occasionally: after all, it's your overall diet that matters rather than individual meals.

**1  Opposite are the six take-away snacks and meals which came out top in the survey. Study them and answer these questions.**

1  The most expensive take-away has the highest protein content. True or False?
2  Why was the cheapest take-away one of the best?
3  Chicken Chow Mein and Doner kebab with salad are both recommended for weight-watchers. But what essentials do both lack?
4  What was particularly good about the meal at £1.15?
5  It's suggested that a salad should be eaten with the Chicken Tandoori and chapatti. Why?
6  The price of a take-away relates directly to the weight. True or False?

**2  These six people are all going out to get a take-away meal. Which of the take-aways opposite would you advise each to buy? Why? (You may recommend more than one of the snacks/meals per person.)**

**Mr A** has been told to eat food with as little fat as possible.
**Miss B** is on a diet which must include food high in carbohydrates.
**Mrs C** thinks, for some reason, that she should eat food with little or no vitamin C
**Mr D** knows he needs to eat food with quite a high iron content.
**Ms E** is slimming and has to watch her calorie intake very carefully.
**Mrs F** has been advised to eat food with a high calcium content.

O6  **Remember what we have said in other Units about writing notes (pp.15 and 34). Read this example, check back, and then write short notes for the other situations.**

**Example:** You came home early from work but had to go out again. It's your turn to prepare supper for your two flatmates. Leave a note (about 15 words) suggesting they go and get an Indian take-away. You'll refund the money later.

> Sorry, can't get supper. Suggest you get Indian takeaways. Will pay you back later.

1  You drank the last of the orange juice after your flatmates had gone out this morning. You won't be back for a day or two. Leave a note.
2  Your flatmates are continually leaving food on the table after meals. You feel strongly that the 'consumer(s)' should always put food away. Write a suitable message (no more than 10 words) to stick on the door of the fridge.
3  You did the food shopping today while your flatmates were out. As you're going out to an evening class, leave a short note telling them where you have put the essentials.

### Baked potato, cottage cheese and salad
£1.15

| Calories | |
|---|---|
| Fibre | 370 |
| Fat | 6g |
| Protein | 5g |
| Carbohydrate | 23g |
| Calcium | 63g |
| Iron | 100mg |
| Vitamin C | 2mg |
| | 30mg |

Based on a 300g potato with 120g cheese

This take-away had by far the lowest fat content. It's also a good choice for slimmers, although slimmers on low-calorie diets might want to be careful they get enough fibre from their other foods. It provides as much vitamin C as most people need in a day, as well as a useful amount of protein, but little iron. A 25g knob of butter would add about 20g more fat. Cheddar cheese and butter would provide around 530 Calories and more calcium, but about five times the fat (27g).

### Beanburger in a wholemeal bun
£1.07

| Calories | |
|---|---|
| Fibre | 520 |
| Fat | 16g |
| Protein | 22g |
| Carbohydrate | 16g |
| Calcium | 69g |
| Iron | 230mg |
| Vitamin C | 4mg |
| | 18mg |

Figures are for a Wimpy beanburger, 236g

Of the take-aways in the survey, this was easily the one with the most fibre – more than half the recommended amount for one day (see 'Your daily needs'). There's also around half the recommended daily amount of vitamin C and calcium. It's a shame more of the large burger chains don't sell beanburgers – we only found them in Wimpy and Casey Jones (see opposite). Chips would increase the fat content, which isn't particularly low anyway.

### Chicken Chow Mein
£2.20

| Calories | |
|---|---|
| Fibre | 390 |
| Fat | 5g |
| Protein | 22g |
| Carbohydrate | 19g |
| Calcium | 28g |
| Iron | 48mg |
| Vitamin C | 2mg |
| | Very low |

Based on a portion weighing 280g

Slimmers will like the low calorie content of this meal (based on chicken, noodles, bean sprouts and bamboo shoots), although the fat content is fairly high in proportion to the number of calories. Make sure you get more calcium, iron and vitamin C from the other things you eat, and you may want to watch your fat intake from other foods, too.

### Chicken tandoori and chapatti
£3.50

| Calories | |
|---|---|
| Fibre | 670 |
| Fat | 4g |
| Protein | 17g |
| Carbohydrate | 81g |
| Calcium | 52g |
| Iron | 97mg |
| Vitamin C | 5mg |
| | — |

Based on 290g of chicken and a 120g chapatti

The chicken provides lots of protein – more than most people's daily requirement. The fat content is low in relation to the calorie count (and much lower than that of fried chicken), but so is the fibre content. There's no vitamin C, either – some salad would help with this.

### Dahl and boiled rice
£1.80

| Calories | |
|---|---|
| Fibre | 690 |
| Fat | 11g |
| Protein | 11g |
| Carbohydrate | 23g |
| Calcium | 132g |
| Iron | 40mg |
| Vitamin C | 6mg |
| | — |

Based on a 330g dahl with 320g of rice

Lots of fibre (dahl is mainly boiled lentils) in this Indian take-away, and very low fat content in relation to the number of calories. It also provides half the iron most people need in a day and a useful amount of protein. But there's little calcium and no vitamin C; a lassi (Indian yoghurt drink) and a salad would help.

### Doner kebab with salad
£1.40

| Calories | |
|---|---|
| Fibre | 405 |
| Fat | 3g |
| Protein | 21g |
| Carbohydrate | 21g |
| Calcium | 36g |
| Iron | 79mg |
| Vitamin C | 3mg |
| | 12mg |

Based on 60g pitta bread with 65g of lamb.

Another take-away for those watching their weight. But the white pitta bread doesn't provide much in the way of fibre; nor is there much calcium or iron here. You'd need to make sure you got enough of these nutrients from the other foods you eat, and you might keep an eye on your fat intake at the same time.

*A1*　**In Unit 8, you took part in a telephone conversation based on a Situations Vacant advertisement. Here is another exercise like that.**

**You are working in a take-away restaurant and have to take telephone orders. You are going to take part in a telephone conversation with a caller. But before you listen to the tape, study the menu in detail and answer the questions below:**

# CHOOSY
# TAKEAWAY RESTAURANT

❋✻❋✻❋✻❋✻❋✻❋✻❋✻❋✻❋✻❋✻❋✻❋✻❋✻❋✻❋✻❋✻❋✻❋✻❋

## STARTERS

| | | | |
|---|---|---|---|
| Prawn cocktail | £1.75 | Tomato soup | £1.30 |
| Chicken noodle soup | £1.30 | Chicken liver pâté | £1.50 |

## MAIN DISHES　Choose any combination!

| | | | |
|---|---|---|---|
| Roast chicken (portion) | £2.20 | Chips (per portion) | .90 |
| Roast spare ribs | £1.75 | Baked potato | .75 |
| Chicken pie | £1.30 | Rice (boiled) | £1.10 |
| Chicken and mushroom pie | £1.30 | Rice (fried) | £1.30 |
| Steak and kidney pie | £1.30 | Pilau rice | £1.30 |
| Steak and mushroom pie | £1.30 | Vegetables (per portion) | .75 |
| Beef or Chicken curry | £2.50 | (peas, carrots, beans, aubergine, | |
| Chicken tandoori | £2.50 | courgettes, braised onions) | |
| Doner kebab – filled | £1.90 | **Salads** | |
| Beefburger in a bun | £1.40 | Green salad | £1.20 |
| Pizza (made to order) | £2.30 | Tomato salad | £1.00 |

## ICE CREAMS

Homemade ice cream (vanilla, strawberry, mint,
blackberry, fudge, cassata, chocolate) (per portion)　　　　　　£1.00

❋✻❋✻❋✻❋✻❋✻❋✻❋✻❋✻❋✻❋✻❋✻❋✻❋✻❋✻❋✻❋✻❋✻❋✻❋

1  What do starters cost?
2  How much do pies cost?
3  What's the least you can spend?
4  What are the cheapest main dishes?

5  What are the most expensive?
6  What kind of choice is there in the
   following: rice? potato? pies?
   salads? vegetables? ice cream?

*A2*　**Now look at the menu, listen and take part in the conversation.**

**A3**

In Units 2 and 7 we concentrated on the following features when reading aloud:

a) numbers/figures;  b) abbreviations;  c) strong and weak forms of words like *of, that, from, had*, etc;  d) tag questions;  e) lists

**Each of the following items shows two or more of the above features. Note down what features each shows (e.g. b + e), listen to them on tape, and then practise reading them aloud yourself:**

1  There can't be more than 300-400 calories in that, can there?
2  We'll need a loaf of bread, a lettuce, some cheese and some tomatoes.
3  Certain EEC regulations already control the use of additives in food.
4  Look what's in this packet soup: dried vegetables (cabbage and carrots, mushroom, onions, parsnips, green peas ...) – The list's endless!
5  You couldn't help me with this maths problem, could you? We've got to work out the area of a room measuring 5.35m by 6.25m.

**A4**

**Study this dialogue, listen to it on cassette, and then read and practise it in pairs:**

MIKE: You're not going to make and eat that, are you?

CAROL: What are you talking about?

MIKE: That packet mix for cheesecake. It *is* for cheesecake, isn't it?

CAROL: Yes, it is. And why shouldn't I make it and eat it? I thought it looked quite nice.

MIKE: Have you read the list of ingredients?!

CAROL: No, I never bother to look at them.

MIKE: You should do. Just listen to what's in this mixture. 'Sugar, cheese powder, vegetable oil, modified starch, emulsifiers (E477, E322), lactose, gelling agents (E339, E450a), whey powder, flavourings, fumaric acid, salt, colours (E102, E110, E160a) and antioxidant (E320).' Sounds disgusting, doesn't it?

CAROL: Yes, it does. But it's all right to eat, isn't it?

MIKE: Some people would say it isn't – especially with all those 'E's in it.

CAROL: They're additives, aren't they?

MIKE: Yes, and some of them are harmless. They help preserve the food. But I know for sure that some of them can be harmful. For instance, I noticed E102 under the colours.

CAROL: Well?

MIKE: E102 stands for tartrazine and it can have all kinds of side-effects. I've got a book here on 'E's. You can look it up yourself.

CAROL: Yes, here it is. "Adverse effects: Susceptible people, especially those sensitive to aspirin, and asthmatics, are sensitive to tartrazine. Reactions include urticaria (skin rashes), rhinitis (hay fever), bronchospasm (breathing problems), blurred vision and purple patches on the skin. It has recently been suggested that tartrazine in fruit cordials may be responsible for wakefulness in small children at night." Well, well!

MIKE: Quite. I think you should get a copy of the book. It's only £2.95, and worth every penny in peace of mind!

CAROL: Yes, I will. And I don't think I'll make that cheesecake after all!

# UNIT 11 Weird and Wonderful

A scene from *Ghostbusters*

## WARM-UP

**Have you seen any of these films?**

*Frankenstein   Dracula
Rosemary's Baby   Omen   Ghostbusters
Alien   An American Werewolf in London*

**If you have, tell the class your impressions. What do you think of horror films and films that exploit our fears of the unknown?**

*A1*   **With a partner, make a list of the things you need to remember when preparing to tell a story from pictures. Refer back to Units 3 (pages 20-21) and 6 (pages 42-43). Then look at the picture story opposite and do exercises A2-A7.**

*A2*   **With a partner, make a list of words you might need when telling the story.**

*A3*   **Listen to the story two or three times. Then tell the story yourself beginning 'A couple of years ago Tony and Carol had a very strange experience.'**

*A4*   **Look at the way we can respond to a comment using *So ...* or *Nor ...***

> Tony was horrified when he read it.   He just didn't believe it!
> So was Carol.   Nor did Carol.

**Now listen to the cassette and make similar comments about the story.**

*A5*   **Look at the way we can agree with people, this time using short tags:**

> It was really strange.   You don't expect anything like that.
> Yes, it was, wasn't it?   No, you don't, do you?

**Now listen to the cassette and react in a similar way.**

*A6*   **In one of the exercises in the ARELS Higher exam you might have to 'transform' sentences beginning with words given, like this:**

> Tony was nearly run over, but the man shouted a warning. (*If the man ...*)
> *If the man hadn't shouted a warning, Tony would/might have been run over.*

**Listen to two more examples, then do the rest. They are all about the picture story.**

A7 Two people, A and B, are talking about the story. Notice how B picks up certain words in A's remarks and then 'goes one better'.

> A: It was strange, wasn't it?
> B: 'Strange'?! It was really weird!
>
> A: It was quite a nice day.
> B: 'Quite nice'?! It was a glorious day!

**Now listen and respond to more remarks about the story in the same way.**

*O1*　**The building opposite is the new Louvre pyramid in Paris. A daily newspaper asked five experts and a few 'men in the street' to comment on it. They were:**

- Benjamin Broadbent, architectural adviser to several cathedral cities
- Ben Lincoln, a community architect
- Martin Bayles, architecture correspondent of a daily newspaper
- Linda Sunderland, an exhibition organiser
- Jean Bolais, president of an institute of French architects
- Joe Public, i.e. a sample of ordinary people.

**Read the set of opinions below the photo. Which one do you agree with most?**

*O2*　**These six people also made some off-the-cuff comments about the building. Match these six comments with the written opinions opposite.**

1 I have mixed feelings; something's been lost and I suppose something gained; offensive it certainly isn't.
2 The aspect of transparency and translucence was much exaggerated, admittedly mainly by the Sunday papers; the claims for framed views of the Palace building and so on are garbage.
3 The detailing I liked a lot, extremely bold. And the feeling of freedom and expanse is exhilarating.
4 For me it shows how much we have to learn from our cross-Channel friends. London could do with more examples of this kind of vision.
5 I wouldn't say it was ugly exactly, but then again it's not the most appealing piece of architecture I've ever seen. What riles me is the inordinate fuss everybody's made about it, all the hype that's been going on around it and the question of who's going to foot the bill.
6 A modest success, but overshadowed by some of its contemporaries, which demand much more serious critical attention.

*O3*　**Now decide whether these statements about the text opposite are True or False. Check your answers with a partner and then the class.**

1 Mr Broadbent is the most enthusiastic of the six about the pyramid.
2 Mr Lincoln is put off by the size of the pyramid.
3 Ms Sunderland is critical of British attitudes to architecture.
4 The man in the street accepts that the building was worth the money spent.
5 Mr Bayles was impressed by the effect of light inside the pyramid.
6 Ms Sunderland suggests that the British are not very interested in architectural matters.
7 Ms Sunderland compares architects to carbuncles.
8 M. Bolais feels this is a symbol of how far French architecture has progressed.
9 Ms Sunderland has a more positive view of the pyramid than M. Bolais.
10 There is some nostalgia in Mr Lincoln's comments.
11 Mr Broadbent hardly noticed the cheap materials used in the construction.
12 The simple forms of the pyramid impressed M. Bolais.

**BENJAMIN BROADBENT** Most impressive; immaculate finish. I adored the massive spans of the central underground space. Impossible to guess that the the ceiling is in-situ concrete and not marble. It's not the pyramid that upsets me, it's its location.

**BEN LINCOLN** I regret the passing of the trees in the court-yard; they somehow helped to disguise the false geometry of the old Palace and the surroundings. Overall, I feel the pyramid is fine in its space; it seems no larger than a kind of fountain. I don't think it detracts from the Palace. Weird, maybe, but also in a way quite wonderful.

**MARTIN BAYLES** Most disappointing is the glass itself. After all the talk of the prismatic effect of it, one enters with high expectations, only to find the walls rather opaque, especially when looking out of the corners. Internal reflections and the fine spray from the nearby fountains conspire to give the impression of dirty acrylic.

**LINDA SUNDERLAND** In England this would be considered a carbuncle, the architect a charlatan and those who built it cowboys. There discussion of architecture is led by media pandering to royal conservatism and architectural matters are discussed, if at all, only in pejorative and clichéd terms. In Paris it's different.

**JEAN BOLAIS** It pales into insignificance, architecturally speaking, compared to the Grande Arche at Tête Défence. That has a kind of stunning simplicity, with its four enormous post-tensioned frames, stabilised by those diagonal walls at the corners. The pyramid is child's play, by comparison; can't see what all the fuss was about. Certainly doesn't deserve the publicity it's received.

**JOE PUBLIC** I resent the money that's been spent, not only on the construction itself, but on the hordes of visitors who've been brought here and wined and dined at the tax-payer's expense, and all for what? To gawp at something that gets in the way of something that was really wonderful.

*04*   In the Oxford Higher, you will have to write a 250-word composition; it may be a narrative, a description or an argument of some kind.
Imagine you are asked to write a description of an unusual building that has made a great impression on you. Weird or wonderful? Where do you start?

The right answer is probably with some notes that form a plan. What are you going to say? How? And in which order? Take five minutes to write that plan NOW.

Did your plan look something like this? And did it answer these questions?

Para 1   Where is the building located? What's near it? What sort of building is it?
Para 2   When was it built? Who by? What for? How has it changed over the years? Has it been renovated? Extended?
Para 3   What does it look like in general? How many floors has it got? Interior as well as exterior description. What style is it in? What materials is it made of? How is it decorated/furnished inside?
Para 4   What special characteristics has it got? What does it remind me of? What makes it special? Attractive? Unattractive? What are its good/bad points?
Para 5   Personal comment on what it means to me. Happy memories or daily disgust? Fear? Unease? Hopes for the future? Stand forever? Be pulled down soon?

*05*   How could such questions be answered in good, semi-formal English? Study this language, then write the description in about 250 words.

We could do with some constructive use of the passive:

The palace was built in the late seventeenth century ...
The castle was mysteriously destroyed by fire in 1566 ...
Recently a great many renovations have been made ...
The gardens have been converted into a safari park ...

Relative pronouns could play a major part. Which of these clauses connect with the openings above?

... , which have destroyed some of the building's original charm.
... , where visitors can mingle with all manner of wildlife.
... by a certain Harvey Wallbuckle, who has haunted the place ever since.
... , when the country was ravaged by civil war.

Participles, present and past, will also have their place, along with adverbs:

... a tastefully furnished lounge adjoining fully equipped kitchens ...
... French windows leading on to a terrace laid out for cocktails ...
... breathtaking chandeliers hanging from low oak-beamed ceilings ...
... fitted carpets, fitted wardrobes, hidden passages, winding staircases ...

*06*   Now plan, make notes for, and write this 250-word composition:

Describe, as for a magazine article, a visit to a museum or art gallery. Mention in some detail a few of the unusual works of art or exhibits that catch your eye and comment on your overall impression.

07  **In the Oxford Higher, you may have to write short notices, signs or labels. To help you do this, read this extract from a ghost story and fill in the gaps.**

I drew up outside the house and found my hand slightly trembling as I put on the handbrake. There were signs everywhere in Gothic script; several on the lawns saying: '**Keep ___ ___ ___**' and a large one saying '**Keep _____**' in front of two large garage doors. I noticed, too, that one or two doors had a large '**Keep _____**' on them.

I walked up to the imposing front door. Glancing down, I saw two empty milk bottles and a handwritten note saying '**No milk today; gone _____**'. There was a notice on the front door: '**Knock and _____** '. I did.

Inside there was a smell of year-old dust and I could see cobwebs hanging from every beam. On a table in front of me, there was a parcel with a label that read: '**Fragile! Handle with _____** .' On it someone had written: '**Not known at this _____ – Return to _____** .' The postmark was December, 1898. I felt a shudder shoot through me. On the other side of the table there was a silver plate with a few copper coins on it and a small card placed against it: '**All contributions will be gratefully _____ . Please _____ generously.**' I passed by. In front of me there was another door which I assumed led to the kitchens. There was a notice stuck on it that read: '**Closed due to staff _____** .' Despite all the written signs, I had still not detected any sign of life. A board that read: '**Wet _____** ' was placed by a wall that was thick with dust and clearly had not been redecorated this century.

I walked up the dark oak staircase to the first floor. On the first door I came to there was a notice saying: '**Do not _____ !**' On the next there was a note that read: '**Quiet please. Conference in _____ .**' I pushed the door open. Inside there was a large oval table with about a dozen chairs around it, papers on it and a grandfather clock standing beside it. On the table there was a small hand-written sign: '**Back in five _____ .**' There were a number of enormous, heavy-looking books chained to the wall in a locked cabinet with the entirely unnecessary instruction printed on a card above them: '**Do not ____ .**' I looked closely at the clock. Someone had pinned a notice on the side of it: '**Out of _____ .**'

I left the room and made for the second staircase. I saw a notice: '**_____ of the _____**', and heard a distant barking. There was also what I first took to be grafitti on the wall but which on closer inspection turned out to be a useful warning: '**Attention! The fifth stair is _____ .**'

I negotiated the absent stair and reached the top of the building. In front of me was a laboratory shelf with a number of bottles on it. The labels read: '**Not to be taken _____ !**', '**Poison!** ,**_____ well before use**' and '**Do not exceed prescribed _____ !**'.

Suddenly I heard .....

# UNIT 12 Problems and Solutions

**Problems! Problems! – In pairs or small groups discuss and suggest a number of possible solutions to these problems. How can you/we**

■ overcome shyness?
■ break personal habits, such as biting your nails?
■ move a car or van which has got stuck in deep mud or sand?
■ solve the problem of increasing traffic in towns and cities?
■ ensure a fairer distribution of wealth, nationally and internationally?

_O1_　**1　Below are some common 'do-it-yourself' and houshold problems together with some _Sunday Times_ 'Guide Lines' telephone numbers to ring for free expert advice on how to deal with them. Read the list, read the problems various people have (top of page 75), then say or write down which numbers they should ring. (As all numbers begin 0898 666, just give the final three digits.)**

**THE SUNDAY TIMES**

**GUIDE LINES**

_Advice by phone_

Keeping household costs down is getting harder all the time. Doing simple repairs and improvements yourself is the most popular way, but there are some jobs that still require expert handling.

We show you which these are, how to get the best people to handle them, and also how to tackle the work you can do yourself.

## DIY/Household

| | |
|---|---|
| Mending leaking pipes | 0898 666 075 |
| Keeping drains clear | 0898 666 076 |
| Clearing blocked sinks | 0898 666 077 |
| Electrical fuses: extra care needed | 0898 666 078 |
| Installing a phone extension | 0898 666 079 |
| Electrical faults you can cure | 0898 666 080 |
| Dealing with fire hazards | 0898 666 081 |
| Leaking roofs: not a DIY job | 0898 666 082 |
| Broken windows: putty and patience | 0898 666 083 |
| Home security: beating the burglar | 0898 666 084 |
| Double glazing can be cheap | 0898 666 085 |
| Tips on home decorating | 0898 666 086 |
| Preparing for DIY | 0898 666 087 |
| Stains in carpets and fabric | 0898 666 088 |
| Stains on clothing | 0898 666 089 |
| Dealing with smells | 0898 666 090 |
| Saving energy: and money | 0898 666 091 |
| Getting rid of damp | 0898 666 092 |
| House plants need your care | 0898 666 093 |
| Saving food leftovers | 0898 666 094 |
| Preventing draughts | 0898 666 095 |
| Storing your goods | 0898 666 096 |
| Furniture cleaning tips | 0898 666 097 |
| Saving time around the house | 0898 666 098 |
| Spring-cleaning without tears | 0898 666 099 |

1 'I've got little paint spots on my skirt.'
2 'The fluorescent light in the kitchen keeps flickering.'
3 'Cooking for one is not much fun and there's so much waste.'
4 'It'd be nice to be able to make calls from the second bedroom.'
5 'The baby spilt milk all over the carpet! What can I do about it?'
6 'I've just got to do something about these astronomical fuel bills.'
7 'There's a large mouldy patch in the corner of the kitchen.'
8 'Are locks on the windows enough, or do we need an alarm system?'

**2 Work in pairs: student A tells student B a DIY or household problem that he or she has; student B consults the list (bottom of page 74) and suggests which 'Guide Lines' number he or she should ring for free advice.**

*O2* **You work for a company that produces powder for automatic dishwashers and have received a letter from an irate user. Here are two paragraphs from the letter:**

'The first time I used the machine with your powder, all my dinner and pudding plates came out with bits of food still sticking on them. (I had to wash everything a second time by hand.) And not only that, glasses and cutlery were all stained and streaky when they came out, too.

 'What is more worrying, however, is that only yesterday I put some hand-painted cups and saucers in to wash with six bone-handled tea knives and was horrified at the result. Some of the hand-painting had worn off, and there were slight cracks in several of the handles.'

**Referring to the directions printed clearly on the side of the packet of powder (right), answer the letter politely (in 150-200 words), pointing out the things users should and shouldn't do. Start some of your sentences with these:**

We were sorry to ...
Whilst we sympathise ...
We take great pains to stress that ...
It is (however) with regret that we are
 unable to ...
It may have escaped your attention ...

# finish

## DIRECTIONS FOR PERFECT RESULTS

**1.** Remove food scraps. If the dishes are going to stand for some time before washing, rinse heavily soiled items. If your dishwasher has a rinse programme this will be ideal.

**2.** Stack your dishwasher carefully according to the manufacturer's instructions. Ensure that all surfaces will be exposed to the water spray.

**3.** Use 1 level scoop of detergent in the dispenser. Never sprinkle directly over the dishwashing. In very hard water areas, or for machines without a water softener, or for very dirty dishes, use more Finish.

**4.** Keep your Finish powder in perfect condition by closing the bag with the twist tie, and store in a dry place.

**5.** The rinse aid dispenser should always be filled with Finish Rinse Aid – check and top it up regularly.

**6.** Use Finish Dishwasher Salt to regenerate the water softener unit.

**7.** Keep your machine at peak efficiency by using Finish Dishwasher Cleaner and Freshener once every three months.

## DISHWASHING TIPS

**DELICATE GLASSWARE:** Use a gentle or economy programme.

**CUTLERY:** Do not mix different metals such as stainless steel and silver in the same compartment.

The intensive nature of automatic dishwashing is unsuitable for some items. If in doubt check with the manufacturer or test one piece for a few weeks. We would not recommend washing the following:
– Some lead crystal and decorated glassware.
– Antique and hand painted porcelain and dishes with patterns over the glaze.
– Cutlery and handles of bone, wood or some plastics, and some grades of silver plate.
– Coloured or anodised aluminium ware.
– Plastic utensils which cannot withstand dishwasher temperatures of around 70°C.

*O3*  **Below right are three diagrams showing the drinking, smoking and viewing habits of teenagers in Britain in the late 1980s. On the left you can read how the first diagram led to a journalist's article. Study the diagrams and read the article, then do the two exercises that follow.**

In the survey, 47 per cent of boys and 34 per cent of girls aged 11 said they had had an alcoholic drink in the previous week. That percentage rose to 72 per cent of boys and 65 per cent of girls aged 15 and 16.

Many youngsters seemed to be regular wine drinkers and the most popular source of alcohol is the home, although nearly a third of those aged 11 and 12, rising to more than half of those aged 15 and 16, had visited a public house in the previous two weeks.

The average weekly consumption for boys aged 14 is seven to eight units (a pint of beer or a glass of wine equals one unit), rising to 8.5 in the North-east.

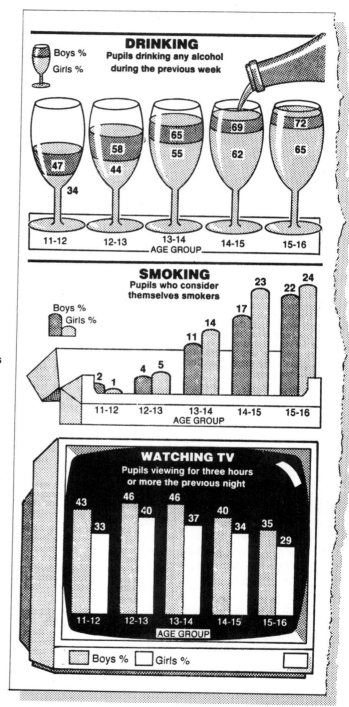

1  **Note carefully the kind of language used in the article above and write three paragraphs to go with the diagram about Smoking. You may want to invent more details. Imagine you work for a popular newspaper that likes to sensationalise the facts. Consider using some of this language:**

Government ministers were horrified to learn that ...
as many as / no fewer than / a staggering 23% / virtually one in four
Believe it or not, ... / Incredible as it might seem, ... / Amazingly enough, ...
Most disturbing of all is the revelation that ...

**2** Now write three paragraphs about the third diagram as part of a letter to a local newspaper. You write as a parent to express your concern – not only about the number of hours young people are spending in front of television sets but also about the sort of programmes they are watching. Before you begin writing, list with a partner the kinds of programme that cause you most concern (and give examples), for instance:

soap operas e.g. 'Dallas'          (adult) situation comedies e.g. ............
game shows e.g. ................          horror films e.g. ...........................

**04**     **Problem: You need to be rescued by air. How do you send messages to a helicopter or an aircraft? Below are some drawings from a Survival manual illustrating what to do in such an emergency. The pictures should be self-explanatory but you are asked to write a sentence for each. For example:**

If you need to signal to an aircraft that you want to be picked up, stand with your legs apart, raise both arms above your head and hold the position.

Some of these words and expressions might be useful:

| | |
|---|---|
| (verbs) | lie  stand  crouch  swing  wave  stretch  clasp |
| (adverbs) | to and fro    up and down    backwards and forwards |
| | from side to side    with your arms outstretched    with your knees |
| | bent    with your hands by your side    with your legs together |

And you might need to use these variations on basic *if* - clauses:

If you have to/If you should need to ... ,    Should you want/need (him) to ... ,
In the event of you(r) needing/having (to) ... ,

**BODY SIGNALS**

This series of signals will be understood by airmen and can be used to signal to them. Note the changes from frontal to sideways positions and the use of leg and body posture as well as hand movements. Use a cloth in the hand to emphasize the YES and NO signals. Make all signals in a clear and exaggerated manner.

| Pick us up | Need mechanical help | Land here | All is well | Have radio |
|---|---|---|---|---|

| YES | NO | Do NOT attempt to land here | Need medical assistance | Use drop message |
|---|---|---|---|---|

*A1*   **Dictionary work and Reading aloud**

One annoying aspect of English (for learners) is that it possesses a number of words of very similar meaning which are not interchangeable in all situations. Here are some words on the subject of problems and solutions:

quandary predicament loss difficulty   trouble mess mind
decision answer decisiveness clue idea brainwave

1   **Use an English-English dictionary (and your own experience and knowledge) to place each of the words above in this passage.**

I'm in a rather nasty (1) ...  at the moment actually and I'm at a (2) ...  to know what to do. You see, the company's in big (3) ...  and I don't really think we can afford my secretary and her mistakes any longer. I have (4) ... in telling people they're not needed any more at the best of times, but she's been with me for nearly ten years! I'm in a (5) ...  as to whether to get rid of her or keep her on just for old times' sake. I don't know what the (6) ...  is! I know I'll have to come to a  (7) ...  soon but I just can't make up my (8) ... . (9) ...  was never my strong point. Does she realise she's a handicap now with all the new technology? I haven't a (10) ... . Would she perhaps be relieved if she had to go?  I haven't the foggiest (11)... . The situation is a complete (12) ... ! I was hoping you might have a (13)... . No? Oh well.

2   **Use a dictionary again to check, if necessary, the pronunciation of these words. Note particularly where the main stress is. We've done the first two for you.**

pre**dic**ament   **ac**tually   difficulty   quandary   decision   decisiveness
handicap   technology   clue   relieved   foggiest   brainwave

3   **Now listen to the passage on cassette, then read it out loud to a partner.**

*A2*   1   **You're going to hear part of an interview with Chris Windley talking about the time he took part in an 'escape and evade' exercise in Scotland when he was a young trainee naval officer. As in the ARELS examination, listen first to get used to the voice and to get a general idea of what he is talking about. Then you will hear the piece again interrupted by detailed questions.**

**As you listen the first time, try to find the answers to these questions:**

1  What do you learn about the exercise?
2  Was it outdoors or indoors?
3  How long did it last?
4  The aim of the exercise was to simulate – what?

2   **Before you listen again, think carefully about what you heard and try to predict some of the questions you might be asked. Write down four or five.**

3   **Now listen again and this time try to answer the questions as they are asked on tape. Afterwards, discuss how good your predictions were.**

*A3*   **1 Look at these two examples of typical ARELS sentence transformations, and then discuss with a partner the best transformations for sentences 1-5. They all have something to do with problems of various kinds.**

There are a lot of road accidents because people don't think enough when they're driving. (If people  ... )
   *If people thought more when they were driving, there wouldn't be so many road accidents.*

Unemployment causes a lot of domestic problems. (A lot of  ... )
   *A lot of domestic problems are caused by unemployment.*

   1 I always find it difficult to give advice about money problems. (I always have ...)
   2 No one seems to be able to solve the problem. (The problem seems ... )
   3 Stricter laws would mean less violence in our streets. (If ... )
   4 Young people have nowhere to go in the evenings. (We need ... )
   5 The problem of football hooliganism can't be easily solved. (There's no ...)

   **2 Now listen to the cassette and do more items like this.**

*A4*   **Giving a short persuasive talk on a prepared topic**

   **Here is a selection of topics related to the themes of Units 9-12 on which you might be asked to make a prepared speech in the examination. Read them carefully, choose one, write brief notes, then be prepared to give a two-minute talk on your topic to a small group or the class.**
   **IMPORTANT: You should refer back to the guidance in Unit 4, pages 30-31.**

   **1** Persuade a friend to have his or her car converted for the use of unleaded petrol in preference to conventional leaded petrol.

   **2** We should all become vegetarians.

   **3** If our great-grandparents could come back and visit us in the 1990s, they'd suffer immediate and serious culture shock.

   **4** What, in your opinion, is the greatest problem facing your own country at this present time? And how do you think it can be solved?

# OXFORD PRACTICE EXAM

# THE OXFORD EXAMINATION IN ENGLISH AS A FOREIGN LANGUAGE

## Higher Level • Paper 1

Time allowed: $2\frac{1}{2}$ hours

Candidates should attempt ALL the questions

All answers must be written in INK or in BIRO

IMPORTANT: Write all your answers for this Practice Exam on separate paper

An English-English dictionary may be used

**Remember that you may use your English-English dictionary**

**1** Write on **ONE** of the following topics in **about 250 words:**

**Either (a)**

You recently attended a music concert or festival (rock, jazz, folk or classical). Write a letter to a friend who shares the same musical tastes as you, telling him or her about the event and saying how it did or did not live up to your expectations.

**Or (b)**

Write an article for your quarterly college magazine, *The World About Us*, to accompany these graphic representations (right). The article should first summarise the information that is presented in the diagrams and then go on to suggest how these trends, if continued, might have repercussions on our everyday life.

*(You are advised to spend no more than 55 minutes on this question.)*

# Traditional families are on the decline

A Census Bureau report out Monday shows a marked decline in the percentage of traditional families – married couples with children – since 1970. The smaller family size in some part is due to both men and women marrying later.

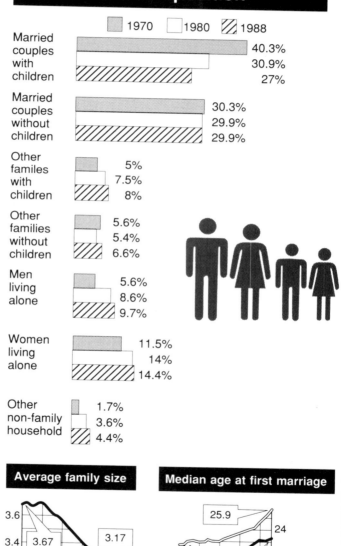

**Household composition**

|  | 1970 | 1980 | 1988 |

Married couples with children — 40.3% / 30.9% / 27%

Married couples without children — 30.3% / 29.9% / 29.9%

Other familes with children — 5% / 7.5% / 8%

Other families without children — 5.6% / 5.4% / 6.6%

Men living alone — 5.6% / 8.6% / 9.7%

Women living alone — 11.5% / 14% / 14.4%

Other non-family household — 1.7% / 3.6% / 4.4%

**Average family size**
3.6, 3.4, 3.2, 3.0, 0 — 3.67, 3.17 — '60 '88

**Median age at first marriage**
25.9, 24, 22, 20, 18, 0 — Men, Women 23.6 — '65 '88

**Remember that you may use your English-English dictionary**

2 You recently helped to organise a protest meeting about the closure of two primary schools in the town where you are at present living. It was a generally peaceful, quite well-behaved affair in which you think many valid points were made. The following Friday the article opposite appeared in your local newspaper (*The Evening Star*). In your anger you marked the article heavily and made comments on a number of things you disagreed with and which you thought were either untrue or unfair.

(i) Write a **letter** to *The Evening Star* complaining about the inaccurate reporting and biassed views expressed in the article and correcting the factual errors it contained.

**(About 250 words.)**

(ii) A good friend who sympathises with your 'cause' unfortunately could not attend the meeting because she is still recovering in hospital from an operation. Write her a **letter** telling her what happened and enclosing a copy of the article.

**(About 120 words.)**

(iii) Write a **short letter** to the owner of the hotel, apologising again for the damage done during the meeting and enclosing a cheque for the amount of compensation you agreed on afterwards.

**(About 80 words.)**

*(You are advised to spend about 60 minutes on this question.)*

**Remember that you may use your English-English dictionary**

# SCHOOLS' PROTEST
# FIZZLES OUT
# IN DRIZZLE

**The much-heralded demonstration** to protest at the closure of Twyneham Primary and St John's First Schools turned out to be nothing much more than a damp squib at the Princess Royal Hotel on Wednesday afternoon. And indeed 'damp' was the operative word. The 'Save the Schools' action group had hoped for a turnout of something in excess of 200. In the event there were barely 50 of them – mainly young mothers – who trudged gloomily from the Sports Centre in Blackmore Street to the hotel in Princes Road, uncertain it seemed as to whether placards or umbrellas should take priority in the air. Their dripping banners looked an extremely sorry sight and, one might say, a rather incongruous one in the light of the Council's recent statement that they are definitely going ahead with closure of the two schools.

On arrival at the Princess Royal Hotel the gallant ladies' numbers were swelled somewhat by passing shoppers and vagrants grateful for some shelter from the steady drizzle.

Inside several attempts at rallying speeches were made but it must be said their effect was more than a little diminished by the intermittent failure of the P.A. system and the constant banging of builders renovating the hotel's ballroom and bar. What words could be heard suggested that the ladies were up in arms because their children will have to travel between two and three kilometres to their new school by means of a specially-laid-on, fully sponsored bus-service.

The highlight of what was otherwise a rather dismal afternoon was not the obviously orchestrated attempt at a chanting march around the hotel grounds but the rather comical incident involving one of the leaders of the meeting. As she rose to offer some parting words of wisdom to the assembled company, one grandiloquent, theatrical gesture saw off a splendid standard lamp which shattered in pieces and must have cost the 'movement' at least a three-figure sum.

As the ladies left there were strains of 'We Shall Overcome'. All very sixties. All rather silly.

A Council spokesman confirmed that he had not been invited to speak at the meeting and said he had no comment to make on what had happened.

*At least 80!*

*No one gloomy!*

*King's Road*

*Not definite!*

*Just not true!*

*Broke down once*

*Stopped after 5 mins.*

*Not the only reason*

*only 50%*

*£40 agreed with hotel*

*Why silly?*

*Why the heavy sarcasm throughout?*

**Remember that you may use your English-English dictionary**

3   On a flight to England you meet a tourist from another country and strike up quite a friendship.  On arrival at Heathrow you get an airline official to take, with your camera, some photos of the two of you standing by the plane. You are now sending two copies of those photos to your 'friend'. Write the short note that you send with the pictures.
**(Up to 50 words.)**

   *(You are advised to spend about 15 minutes on this question.)*

4   You are staying in a friend's flat for a weekend while he is away and accidentally knock a framed print off the wall in his hall.  The glass is broken, but the print itself is undamaged. As it's Sunday, you can't do anything about it and have to leave to catch your train in five minutes.  Write the note that you leave for your friend.
**(About 30 words.)**

   *(You are advised to spend about 10 minutes on this question.)*

5   A friend of yours has just failed her driving test for the second time. You send her this card that you've bought, but you don't just want to sign it. Write something encouraging or cheering to go under the printed message.
**(No more than 15 words.)**

   *(You are advised to spend about five minutes on this question.)*

6   You and a friend have written a song and are now putting it onto cassette in the school library. You don't want anyone to come in for the next half an hour.  Write a notice to put on the library door.
**(No more than 10 words.)**

   *(You are advised to spend no more than five minutes on this question.)*

# OXFORD PRACTICE EXAM

## THE OXFORD EXAMINATION IN ENGLISH AS A FOREIGN LANGUAGE

## Higher Level • Paper 2

Time allowed: 2 hours

Candidates should attempt ALL the questions

In order to help you plan your answers, it is suggested that you spend roughly the following times on the questions set:

*1* 30 minutes
*2* 20 minutes
*3* 25 minutes
*4* 45 minutes

Note: The ordering of types of question in this Practice Exam Paper may not be exactly as you would find them in a real Oxford Higher Paper 2.

All answers must be written in INK or in BIRO

IMPORTANT: Write all your answers for this Practice Exam on separate paper

An English-English dictionary may be used

**Remember that you may use your English-English dictionary**

*(You are advised to spend about 30 minutes on this question.)*

1

## SECTION A

Read the text opposite about our eating and food-buying habits and write (below) the twelve words you think are missing from the text.

| | | | | | |
|---|---|---|---|---|---|
| 1 | _____ | 5 | _____ | 9 | _____ |
| 2 | _____ | 6 | _____ | 10 | _____ |
| 3 | _____ | 7 | _____ | 11 | _____ |
| 4 | _____ | 8 | _____ | 12 | _____ |

## SECTION B

Answer these questions about the second half of the text. With 'True or false?' questions, justify your answers

1 Fewer preservatives are required today than, say, five years ago. True or false?

2 Why should bread go mouldy sooner now than it did in recent years?

3 Why, according to the article, have so many artificial colours been used in foodstuffs recently?

4 Are artificial colourings on the increase or decrease?

5 Whether food manufacturers produce more food now with fewer additives is really up to us, the customers. True or false?

6 Even if it were proved that additives were not harmful, many consumers would still be unhappy about buying food with additives in it. True or false?

## SECTION C

Taking your information from the article, write a brief summary (50-60 words) urging people to buy food with fewer preservatives.

**Remember that you may use your English-English dictionary**

# ARE ADDITIVES REALLY NECESSARY?

*" 'I don't use additives at home, so why should food producers use them?' "*

Even if this person's statement were true, there would be good reasons for food producers to use *some* additives. But is the statement true? If you've ever made a Victoria sandwich cake by the all-in-one method, you'll **1** have used sodium bicarbonate (500) and acid sodium pyrophosphate, two of the **2** of baking powder. If you've ever **3** apple to strawberries when making jam, it would not have **4** so much for the flavour as for the E440(a) to help it set. [E440(a) is pectin which is naturally present in quite **5** amounts in apples.] And anyone who has tried to make mayonnaise **6** egg yolk will know that the oil and vinegar just won't mix because there's no lecithin (E322) to emulsify the two. [ Egg yolks naturally contain the emulsifier, lecithin.] The point is that many of the additives used by food producers are naturally-occurring compounds which are simply extracted from other foods.

## THE CHANGING PLACE OF FOOD PREPARATION

There was a **7** when everyone bought food every day and prepared it in the household kitchen. Today, many people shop no more **8** once a week and a great **9** of food preparation has moved from the home to the factory. Distributing food from factories to supermarkets means that it is, inevitably, subjected to temperature **10** and possibly to vibration which wouldn't occur in homemade foods. Both of these make it more **11** that foods which are emulsions (for example mayonnaise, sauces and ice cream) will separate or suffer an adverse change in texture. To help to maintain the **12** possible texture, not only are emulsifiers used to create the emulsion in the first place, but stabilisers help to preserve that emulsion during distribution.

## PRESERVING PRESERVATIVES

In recent years, the whole business of getting food to supermarkets has been speeded up considerably and everyone concerned with distribution has become much more aware of the importance of refrigeration so the need for preservatives to inhibit the growth of micro-organisms has decreased. But it hasn't been eliminated. One of the major reasons why some preservatives are still used in certain foods — particularly meat products — is to ensure that, if food is not stored under ideal conditions after it is sold, the risk of it causing food poisoning is reduced.

Now that a lot of bread is made without preservatives, you may have noticed that it becomes mouldy more quickly. Shoppers have to accept that, if fewer preservatives are used, some foods will go off more quickly and will need to be stored more carefully at home.

## 'COSMETIC' APPEAL

One of the arguments of the anti-additives lobby is that many additives just make food nicer to look at or to taste; they don't help to keep it safe for longer. These colours, flavourings and flavour enhancers are, they say, not necessary. The question is: Not necessary for whom? Certainly food producers have no burning desire to load food with colours. Those that are used are there because not too many people like white margarine, white custard or instant desserts, or brownish-grey canned strawberries.

## CUSTOMER CHOICE

But tastes are changing. Many people now accept almost-white strawberry yogurt and much paler ice creams, which is why such Sainsbury's products no longer have added colouring. If more people would accept colourless boiled sweets, not-very-red raspberry jelly, and other less-highly-coloured foods, more colours could be eliminated from more foods. It really is a matter of customer choice.

Most people agree that additives which keep food safe and wholesome are useful — even necessary. And most consumers would probably also agree that, provided they can be convinced that they are safe, there's no reason why some colours and flavourings shouldn't be used, too. After all, eating should be a pleasure. The question that many consumers are asking is: Are additives safe?

**Remember that you may use your English-English dictionary**

*(You are advised to spend 20 minutes on this question.)*

2 The TV Films guide printed opposite appeared in an issue of the *TV Times*, a weekly magazine for viewers of ITV and Channel 4 in Britain. Use it to answer **ALL THREE** questions in this section.


## SECTION A

Listed below are eight phrases taken from the film reviews. (The films they refer to are given in brackets.) In each case explain briefly what the phrase means and note whether it adds something positive (P) or negative (N) to the review.

1 vigorous comedy-thriller ('Cottage to Let')
2 rather hampered by studio insistence on using old Stan-and-Ollie routines ('The Big Noise')
3 The plot is too slight ('The Thomas Crown Affair')
4 foregrounds do occasionally wobble ('Pete's Dragon')
5 the songs are largely undistinguished ('Pete's Dragon')
6 a vertigo-inducing trio ('Pete's Dragon')
7. a soapy sheen ('John and Yoko: A Love Story')
8 tersely edited ('Touki Bouki')


## SECTION B

Explain the following words and phrases as they are used in the descriptions. (The title of the film in which you can find each word is given in brackets.)

1 the vogue ('Easy Money')
2 a massive win on the pools ('Easy Money')
3 on the loose ('Cottage to Let')
4 glitzy ('The Thomas Crown Affair')
5 a short ('Snow Children')
6 animation ('Pete's Dragon')
7 pretty far-out ('The Rocky Horror Picture Show')
8 a decent imitation ('John and Yoko: A Love Story')


## SECTION C

From the reviews of the twelve films, pick one that you could describe as poor, one as average or mediocre, and one as excellent. Name them and justify your selection using *one brief sentence* for each.

---

**Remember that you may use your English-English dictionary**

*David Quinlan previews
the films and Monty Smith
the TV movies on ITV and C4*

# Films

## SATURDAY 17th

### Easy Money
*C4, 10.30am–12.15pm*
The British became very fond of multiple-story films in the Forties, but the vogue was killed off rather quickly by the advent of half-hour stories on television. This film is about the effect, on four people from varying walks of life, of a massive win on the pools. *1947*

### Cottage to Let
*C4, 2.00pm–3.45pm*
Anthony Asquith's vigorous comedy-thriller about Nazi agents on the loose in Scotland is a splendid piece of fiction of its time. George Cole makes his screen debut at the age of 16 as a cockney evacuee. *1941*

### The Big Noise
*C4, 3.45pm–5.05pm*
One of Laurel and Hardy's last comedies, this one has some inventive ideas, but was rather hampered by studio insistence on using old Stan-and-Ollie routines without any new variations. The duo's fans may spot a small appearance by Edgar Dearing who was the hopping-mad motorcycle cop in their classic *Two Tars*. Here, he's a... motorcycle cop. *1944*

### The Thomas Crown Affair
*ITV, 11.05pm–1.00am*
Thirty years before, this would have starred Kay Francis and been called *Undercover Girl*. In 1968, with the stars making psychedelic love, it seemed a glitzy fuss about not very much. The plot is too slight to allow Steve McQueen and Faye Dunaway to expand their roles enough for us to identify fully

### 'TV version'
Feature films shown on television are not necessarily in the form originally seen in cinemas. Often several variations are made at the time of production for use according to the intended outlet. In some cases cinema versions may be used, with minor cuts for violence, explicit sex and bad language.
*TVM = TVMovie*

with them, although the bank raid scenes are tautly effective, the music's excellent and there's a nice chess/seduction scene reminiscent of the eating orgy in *Tom Jones*. *1968*

### Snow Children
*ITV, 4.05am–4.35am*
Beautifully photographed short capturing the enchanting world of Antarctic penguins. *1970*

## SUNDAY 18th

### Flesh and the Devil
*C4, 2.00pm–4.05pm*
A sensation on its release in 1927, this was Greta Garbo's third American film, and the first in which she played opposite her favourite co-star, the dashing John Gilbert. The love scenes — astonishing for their time — mirrored the famous off-screen romance, sometimes to the embarrassment of director Clarence Brown, who subsequently directed the Swedish superstar in six films. *1927*

### Pete's Dragon
*ITV, 2.30pm–4.55pm*
This Disney musical fantasy combines live action and animation, and very young children will love it. Purists will notice that foregrounds do occasionally wobble, and the songs are largely undistinguished. But the cast has its moments, especially in a vertigo-inducing trio sung by Helen Reddy, Mickey Rooney and youngster Sean Marshall at the top of a lighthouse. *1977*

### A Star is Dead
*ITV, 7.15pm–8.40pm*
Flashbacks help to sort out the facts from fiction in this feature-length mystery featuring the man with no first name: Quincy

(played with brisk good humour by Jack Klugman). The busiest pathologist in the history of crime is here kept company by fellow TV actors Robert Foxworth (star of *Falcon Crest*) and urbane William Daniels (*St Elsewhere*). *TVM 1976*

### The Rocky Horror Picture Show
*C4, 10.00pm–11.55pm*
Hugely successful musical comedy horror, which is pretty far-out even for the mid-Seventies. An all-American couple, unwise enough to stop at a castle to use the phone, are both seduced by its occupant, a transsexual transvestite Transylvanian intent on creating a superman for his own pleasures. The best performance comes from Richard O'Brien (who also wrote it) as the obligatory hunchback. *1975*

### John and Yoko: A Love Story
*ITV, 11.30pm–2.15am*
Portions of 31 songs associated with John Lennon ripple through this American docu-drama serving as a biographical and emotional shorthand as the 14-year affair between the former Beatle and Yoko Ono is given a soapy sheen. Mark McGann (brother of *Monocled Mutineer* star Paul) manages a decent imitation of Lennon, but Kim Miyori is too frail and pretty to convince as Yoko. *TVM 1985*

### Touki Bouki
*C4, 12.55am–2.35am*
This film from Senegal, a partly autobiographical reflection on exile by its director, is constructed as a surrealistic poem. Sharply made, well shot in colour and tersely edited. *1973*

## MONDAY 19th

### My Favourite Blonde
*C4, 9.30am–10.55am*
Nearly all of Bob Hope's films in the comedy-thriller vein were successful, and this was one of the best. It began the 'favourite' series, which continued with *My Favourite Brunette* and *My Favourite Spy*. *1942*

**Remember that you may use your English-English dictionary**

*(You are advised to spend 25 minutes on this question.)*

3   Your school or college library is divided into the following sections:

| | | |
|---|---|---|
| 1  Fiction Authors A-L | 7  Media and Communications | 13  Children's Books |
| 2  Fiction Authors M-Z | 8  Biography | 14  Legal and Financial |
| 3  History | 9  Reference | 15  Politics and Sociology |
| 4  Science and Technology | 10  Educational Books | 16  Travel |
| 5  Arts | 11  Poetry and Plays | |
| 6  Hobbies and Pastimes | 12  Natural World | |

**(a)** You have received the books listed below. Indicate with the relevant number which section you will put them in. You might not use all sections.

Verse and Worse – An Anthology ☐
Do-It-Yourself Conveyancing ☐
The Truth about the Tabloids by James Walker ☐
Kids' Own Annual ☐
The Adventures of Peter Rabbit by Beatrix Potter ☐
Rich: the legend of Richard Burton re-examined ☐
Understanding Algebra ☐
Does Accent Matter?  by John Honey ☐
The Standard Life of a Temporary Pantihose Salesman – a new novel by A. Busi ☐
The Natural Party of Opposition?  – a study by Prof. W. Barnett ☐
Mind Children: The Future of Robot and Human Intelligence ☐
The Past is Myself –  wartime experiences of Christabel Bielenberg ☐
Neighbours: Behind the Scenes of the Soap ☐
Misery – Stephen King – another blockbusting best-selling tale of mystery ☐
Europe on 10 dollars a day ☐
The Mating Habits of Yellow Wagtails ☐

**(b)** With the present expansion of the library, you feel it is time to divide each of the sections above into sub-sections.  Which of the proposed sub-sections below would go into which section above? Indicate again with the respective number.

| | | | |
|---|---|---|---|
| 20th Century European Drama | ☐ | Astronomy | ☐ |
| Science for School Exams | ☐ | Marine Life | ☐ |
| Creative Cookery | ☐ | Between the Wars | ☐ |
| Lexicons and Thesauruses | ☐ | Pre-school reading | ☐ |
| The Press | ☐ | D I Y | ☐ |

**(c)** Write down three more sub-sections for each of these main sections:

**Science and Technology:** _____  _____  _____

**Arts:** _____  _____  _____

**Hobbies and Pastimes:** _____  _____  _____

**Legal and Financial:** _____  _____  _____

**Remember that you may use your English-English dictionary**

*(You are advised to spend 45 minutes on this question.)*

4   You compiled the information overpage with some colleagues. Below are extracts from three letters received from prospective holidaymakers. Using only the information on the following two pages (92-93), write replies to all **three** extracts. Your replies need not be set out as letters.  (Write 100-120 words for each.)

**Letter (a)**

> A party of eight of us (all students) would like to go to Florida next year. We would like a little information about the best time to go, the cheapest way to get there, what to try and see, and a few details about fly-drive.

**Letter (b)**

> Friends of ours who went there for a holiday last year said everything was absolutely marvellous.  It's a little difficult to believe.  Surely there must be some drawbacks.  You've been there, haven't you?  What can you tell us?

**Letter (c)**

> The last time we went abroad, we had all sorts of problems. We got lost in the backstreets of the city, I had my handbag stolen, and I was short of money because we'd only taken cash. We'd love to go to Orlando and Cape Canaveral, but you can see why we're a bit hesitant, can't you? Can you give us any tips on how to avoid such 'disasters' there?

# FLORIDA

**From Mickey Mouse land at Orlando to the shuttle launch pads at Cape Canaveral, big thinking and big money mark out Florida as leisure country, American style.**

The Spaniards called it the fever coast. Property sharks in the 1920's sold off patches of mosquito-ridden swamp to sucker speculators looking for a place in the sun. The crash of 1929 put a finish to that – but not to the string of gaudy hotels rising on Miami beach, nor to Henry Flagler's dream of a railroad running all the way to the tip of the 'Keys' off Florida's south coast, bringing tourists and settlers from the cold north.

Our map shows the southern part of Florida, where, once more, sunshine is drawing the crowds. Families head for Orlando's theme parks while rich retirees warm their ageing bones on the balconies of their 'Adult Community Condominiums'. And on Florida's endless miles of white beach, holidaymakers slowly roast.

## THE BRITS ABROAD

Florida has become the new frontier for British holidaymakers in search of sun and fun. Numbers have doubled since 1986 to over half a million, and where 12 tour operators once went, 38 go today. The lure is the ideal combination of a week's mouse-chasing in Orlando and a week's sun and sand.

## BEFORE YOU LEAP

So should you abandon the beaches of the Med and head across the pond without further thought? Not without considering:

### The Upside

● Florida hotels are generally a step or two up on Mediterranean package hotels. Colour tellies, huge beds, air conditioning and showers in all rooms are more or less standard, whatever the price. There are some fleapits around, but the standard of comfort is generally high.
● The beaches are truly fabulous, especially those on the west coast, which are famous for their sunsets and shells. Public beaches usually have lifeguards.
● The theme park complexes at Orlando provide enough fun and fury for the most energetic family. They go out to entertain, and do it in style.
● There's plenty of opportunity to find packages which will give you a taste of both east and west coast, plus Orlando, or which just rent you a car and let you follow your own inclinations.

### The Downside

● The flight across the Atlantic is long: about 6 or 7 hours. Small children can get bored.
● The entertainment can get costly. Step outside your hotel or eat anything other than fast food, and costs start mounting. Packages already cost around £200 more than their Mediterranean equivalents. You should reckon on a good tranche of spending money on top of this.
● If you go in summer, be prepared for heat, humidity and even hurricanes. In late spring and early autumn, expect torrential rainstorms. Beaches are often shadeless, and stumping the theme parks can be exhausting on a hot day.
● Florida is new country: apart from the modern attractions, the old town of Key West, and the wildlife of the Everglades National Park, there's not a lot to see by way of historical sights or interesting landscape.
● Unless you're prepared to confine yourself to your hotel, or take advantage of bus trips laid on by your tour operator, you'll need a car. In many resorts, the nearest restaurant may be at least a mile away. And some of the 'free car' offers made by many tour ops may be less economical than they seem, once you've paid the vital insurance and taxes.
● With one or two exceptions, Florida beach resorts are unexciting. Most are shapeless bits of ribbon development plonked down on a flat coastline, plagued by traffic and with no discernible centre.
● The State of Florida is very hot on enforcing its 21 age limit for alchohol consumption. If you look vaguely under thirty, you'll have to provide photographic ID.
● America's sun-bathers are a conservative bunch. If you want an all-over tan, don't come here.

*DISNEY WORLD, ORLANDO.*

## PACKAGES

These price-ranges are for 14 night July and August holidays in 1990. They drop fairly substantially for Spring and Autumn. Many packages allow you to split your time between Orlando and the beaches.

### Pricey packages (£1,000 +)

At the top of the range you'll get a trouble-free fortnight in one of Florida's 1920's palace hotels (see resort descriptions for the gems) or in a luxury 'resort hotel' – maybe with security guards at the gates, a golf course and a strip of beach kept as free as possible from intruding outsiders. In Orlando, you can stay at some of Disney's own hotels.

### Medium price (£700-£1000)

In this range, you'll be able to use some of the smarter chain hotels – Hiltons or Sheratons for example. Many of these are extremely pleasant, and often well situated, but it's worth taking the time to choose a pleasant resort. In Orlando, many of the closest hotels to Disney World come into this price category.

### The cheaper end (under £700)

There's a remarkable range of hotels in this price bracket – some excellent, others that are fairly tatty, uninteresting motels. There's limited self-catering. Many hotels are on the fringes of resorts (so you'll certainly need a car). Beware of very cheap deals – the hotel may be a disappointment.

### Fly-drive (from £400)

You can get packages which just give you flight and car, or you can buy accommodation vouchers (from £22 – £50 per room per night) as well. These are either for one hotel chain, or for groups of budget, standard, or superior hotels.

## FLORIDA SURVIVAL

● Florida is big. This applies to the cities as well as to the distances between them. If you're working out your route in advance, plan your driving in easy stages.

● City maps are important. Most petrol stations have a selection. Without one it's easy to get helplessly lost once you leave the main through routes.

● If you're in a big city, it's wise not to stroll around quiet streets after dark, especially if you are your own or look like an obvious tourist.

● Taxes of 6% are added to almost all purchases (and are not shown on menus or price tags). These, plus the usual 15% service tip, can cause an unexpected hole in your budget.

● Take your spending money in US$ travellers' cheques. We never had trouble getting them cashed in hotels or banks. Changing foreign currency (including sterling) is more difficult. A credit card is almost essential.

● If you are reserving a hotel room over the phone in advance, you'll almost always have to give full credit card details. It can be a time-consuming process as can be checking in and out.

### TRAVEL FACTS

**By air** The cheapest scheduled APEX fares to Miami are currently British Airways (£462) and to Orlando, Continental or Pan Am (£481). Look out for special deals and seat-only charters.

**Car hire** from Miami airport in a group A car starts at £68 for one week (not including insurance & taxes). You may find cheaper deals away from airports.

**Internal flights** are good value. Miami to Orlando (one way) costs £23 with Pan Am, and Orlando to Key West £44 with US Air.

**Maps & Books** Rand Macnally publish general maps of Florida and the Miami area (£1.95). City maps can be found in petrol stations. We liked the *Insight guide to Florida* (£10.95) as a good introduction, and the *Fodor's Guide* (£8.95) is useful on the ground.

# ARELS PRACTICE EXAM

## The ARELS Higher Certificate Examination in Spoken English and Comprehension

NOTE: This ARELS Higher Certificate Practice Exam consists of six Sections and will last approximately an hour. These four pages contain all the material that you need to refer to during the Practice Exam.

### SECTION ONE

In this section you have to give a short persuasive talk. Choose ONE of the five TOPICS below and prepare a TWO-MINUTE TALK on it. You have EIGHT MINUTES to prepare your talk and you may make brief notes. You will be allowed to refer to these notes while you are giving your talk. Do not attempt to write out your talk in full.

### Topics
(Remember you may agree or disagree with the topic.)
1  I wouldn't survive on a desert island.
2  We must invest more money in alternative forms of energy.
3  What you do in your leisure time is just as important as your work or studies.
4  With the present state of the world economy, there's no point in saving money.
5  Moral standards are now lower than they have ever been in the past 200-300 years.

### SECTION TWO

#### Part 3

In this part you have to take part in a short telephone conversation. You work for a bookshop called 'English Books'. Your boss is Mr Brown. On the right you see today's page in his diary. He is about to telephone you.

Listen and take part in the dialogue.

THURSDAY 28th

a.m.    Visit Rogers and Rogers, suppliers, all morning.

p.m.    3.30 2.00 Alan Bowen to visit shop - tour of warehouse.
5.00 Interview J. McBride

## SECTION THREE

In this section we test your intonation, stress, rhythm, pronunciation and other details of the way you speak. Your friend Andrew is ringing to remind you about a book on antique clocks you said you'd try to get for him. You'll hear Andrew's part on the tape, and you must read the part marked **CANDIDATE**. You have two minutes to study the passage before you start reading. You may write on it if you like. Remember, you will have to read the part marked **CANDIDATE**.

**Andrew:** *Hello, Pat. It's Andrew. I thought I'd give you a ring to ask you ......*

**CANDIDATE:** Andrew, nice to hear from you. How are you?

**Andrew:** *I'm fine, thanks. How are you?*

**CANDIDATE:** Not too bad, you know. I had a bout of 'flu a week ago, but I've got over it now. There's a lot of it about though, isn't there?

**Andrew:** *You're right, there is. That's why I haven't seen you recently then?*

**CANDIDATE:** Yes, I promised to ring you about that book a couple of weeks ago, didn't I? I haven't forgotten. I just felt too rough to do anything about it.

**Andrew:** *Have you been able to track it down then?*

**CANDIDATE:** Yes, what a job! Anyway, I've got some information here. It's all in a catalogue I get fairly regularly, published by an antiquarian bookseller near London. But the way, the author was Edwardes — spelt with an 'e', wasn't it?

**Andrew:** *Yes, that's right.*

**CANDIDATE:** Well, there are three titles here by Edwardes — with an 'e'. Let me read them out to you and you can make a note of whichever you want.
'Edwardes, E.L.: "The Grandfather Clock", 1980, 215pp, VG — oh, that means very good condition — and the price, £15.' Then there's another here:
'Edwardes, E.L.: "The Story of the Pendulum Clock", 1977, 270pp, VG, £21'.

**Andrew:** *And did you say there's a third?*

**CANDIDATE:** Yes. I'll read it to you. 'Edwardes, E.L.: "Weight-driven Chamber Clocks of the Middle Ages and Renaissance", 1965, 160pp, £12.50'.

**Andrew:** *That's super. Thanks. I've made a quick note of them, so I think I'll contact the shop myself. Have you got the details handy?*

**CANDIDATE:** Yes. It's John Vyne — that's V-Y-N-E. John Vyne, 5, Manshurst Road, ...

**Andrew:** *Sorry, can you spell 'Manshurst'?*

**CANDIDATE:** M-A-N-S-H-U-R-S-T. Manshurst Road, Hightown, post code HT1 3XY. Oh, and the telephone number is 08922-3477.

**Andrew:**      *Thanks very much. I think I'll give them a ring.*

**CANDIDATE:** Do. I've always found them very helpful. – Just before you go,
                Andrew: see you at the game on Saturday?

**Andrew:**      *I wouldn't miss it for the world. Cheers.*

**CANDIDATE:** See you Saturday, then. 'Bye.


## SECTION FOUR

### Question 3

Two business partners (a man and a woman) are discussing the telephone symbol to be used on their headed company notepaper which they are redesigning. Listen to their conversation, then write an 'M' (for man) and a 'W' (for woman) in the two boxes which correspond to the symbols they each prefer.

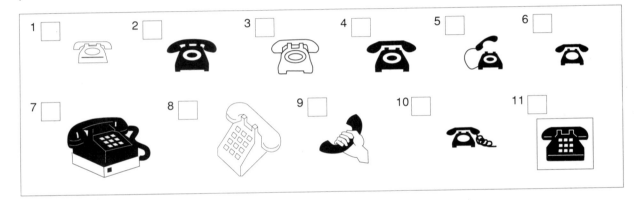

### Question 5

| | | |
|---|---|---|
| **Example**: | He liked the present. | ☐ |
| | He didn't like the present. | ✔ |
| | He likes anything I buy him. | ☐ |
| | | |
| **(a)** | You should have written to him. | ☐ |
| | You should have telephoned *her* . | ☐ |
| | Someone else should have telephoned him. | ☐ |
| | | |
| **(b)** | That's not typical of her. | ☐ |
| | People criticise her for saying silly things. | ☐ |
| | She writes a lot of silly things, too. | ☐ |
| | | |
| **(c)** | I'm sure John didn't tell them. | ☐ |
| | They didn't tell John about it. | ☐ |
| | I assume John told them. | ☐ |
| | | |
| **(d)** | We all enjoyed the party. | ☐ |
| | I thought the party would be terrible. | ☐ |
| | I'm asking: was it a good party? | ☐ |

## SECTION FIVE: PICTURE STORY: The Missing Jewel Box

# Listening Comprehension texts

## UNIT 1    SPORTS AND LEISURE

TUTOR: **Unit 1, Sports and Leisure. Look at page 8, exercise A2. Listen carefully to how the woman agrees with the man. Ready?**

MAN: I'm not very keen on athletics.

WOMAN: Nor am I.

MAN: I've been skiing just once.

WOMAN: So have I.

MAN: I'd never seen synchronised swimming until I saw it in the Olympics.

WOMAN: Nor had I.

MAN: I can play badminton quite well.

WOMAN: So can I.

MAN: I wasn't any good at running when I was at school.

WOMAN: Neither was I.

TUTOR: **Unit 1. Look at page 8, exercise A4. Here are five more statements made by a friend about sport. Agree in the same way, with just three words.**
Eleven.

MAN: I just couldn't go mountaineering. (PAUSE)

WOMAN: Nor could I./Neither could I.

TUTOR: Twelve.

MAN: I'd like to go sailing though. (PAUSE)

WOMAN: So would I.

TUTOR: Thirteen.

MAN: I've never been hang-gliding. (PAUSE)

WOMAN: Nor have I./Neither have I.

TUTOR: ·Fourteen.

MAN: I like watching exciting sports. (PAUSE)

WOMAN: So do I.

TUTOR: Fifteen.

MAN: I went to the new swimming pool at the weekend. (PAUSE)

WOMAN: So did I.

TUTOR: **Unit 1. Look at page 9, exercise A7.** Now you will hear five more situations in which you might find yourself. Say what it seems natural to say in each situation. Ready? Six.

WOMAN: Someone told you yesterday that the school basketball team lost an important match. A

friend of yours plays in the team. What do you say when you see him? (PAUSE)

TUTOR: Seven.

MAN: You've just seen an advertisement in a students' magazine for a cheap fortnight's winter sports holiday in Canada and you would like to go. But you'd like a friend to go with you. What do you say to the friend when you next see him or her? (PAUSE)

TUTOR: Eight.

WOMAN: You've just read in the local paper that a friend of yours has won a tennis championship, so you ring her up. What do you say? (PAUSE)

TUTOR: Nine.

WOMAN: You're talking to three friends. You all think you need some exercise. What do you suggest to them? (PAUSE)

TUTOR: Ten.

WOMAN: A former friend has rung to invite you to see an international football match. You'd like to see the match, but not with him or her. What do you say? (PAUSE)

TUTOR: That's the end of exercise A7 – and the end of the ARELS part of Unit 1.

## UNIT 2    MONEY MATTERS

TUTOR: **Unit 2, Money Matters. Look at page 18, exercise A1.** Listen carefully to this sentence and repeat it.
[As in Students' Book]

TUTOR: **Unit 2. Look at page 18, exercise A2.** Listen to these figures and abbreviations, and repeat them.
[As in Students' Book]

TUTOR: Now listen to the sentences and repeat them.
[As in Students' Book]

TUTOR: **Unit 2. Look at page 19, exercise A3.** Listen to the sentences and repeat them.
[As in Students' Book]

TUTOR: **Unit 2. Look at page 19, exercise A4.**
Look at the dialogue and listen.
[As in Students' Book]

TUTOR: That's the end of exercise A4 – and the end of Unit 2.

## UNIT 3   ENTERTAINMENT

TUTOR: **Unit 3, Entertainment. Look at page 21, exercise A5.** You've already studied the story and thought about what you might say. Remember you have to tell the story in the past, and you must start with the phrase 'One day last month Peter and Maria ...'. Look at the picture story and listen to how one person tells it.

WOMAN: One day last month Peter and Maria were walking along the High Street in their home town when they saw an advertisement for a rock concert. It was 'Triangular Beat'. Maria was really excited because she had always wanted to see the group live. They couldn't read the poster very well, so they crossed the road to have a closer look, and discovered the concert was the next evening. Maria asked Peter if he'd like to go, and when he said yes, they went straight to the theatre box office to get tickets. Luckily there were still plenty of seats left, so they booked two seats fairly near the front – F6 and F7. The concert was due to start at half past seven, so they agreed to meet and catch the bus at a quarter to seven. They didn't live far from the theatre, but they wanted to get there in plenty of time.

The next evening they caught the bus, but the traffic was so heavy that they were still on it at a quarter past seven, and were both getting very worried.

By the time the bus reached the theatre, it was nearly a quarter to eight. They jumped off and ran to the theatre as fast as they could. Maria was afraid they wouldn't be allowed in because they were so late. The concert *had* started – they could hear the noise from outside! – but they were allowed in and led to their seats in row F near the front. Maria thought it was amazing. The

theatre was packed with fans all clapping along to the music – and on stage, *there* was 'Triangular Beat', her favourite group.

They hadn't been in their seats very long when all of a sudden – right at the beginning of one of the group's famous songs – a spotlight started travelling around the audience and stopped on Maria. The lead singer pointed to her and then beckoned her onto the stage. She didn't believe it. She sat rooted to her seat and said to Peter: 'He doesn't mean me, does he?' 'Yes,' said Peter. 'Go on.' And he pushed her out into the aisle. She walked towards the stage in a dream, with the singer shouting all the time: 'Yes, come on. You. Come up here. Come up the side steps.'

The group started the song and Maria, in a complete daze, found herself holding a microphone and singing along with her idol.

She was in a daze then. She was in a daze when they left the concert an hour later, and she was still in a daze the following morning. She just couldn't believe she had been on stage with her favourite group. She actually said she couldn't remember it. But she had to believe it when Peter came round to her house to show her an article and photo in the local newspaper – because there it was in black and white: 'Local Girl Sings With Triangular Beat'.

TUTOR: Run the cassette back and listen to the story again. Then tell it yourself.

TUTOR: **Unit 3. Look at page 21, exercise A7.**
Listen to these sentences about the story. You must complete them using the right form of the phrase 'sing with the group'. We've done the first two for you as examples. Ready?

TUTOR: Example one.
MAN: She really enjoyed ...
... singing with the group.
TUTOR: Example two.
MAN: The lead singer asked Maria ...
... to sing with the group.
TUTOR: One.
MAN: I can't imagine Peter ... (PAUSE)
... singing with the group.

| | |
|---|---|
| TUTOR: | Two. |
| MAN: | No one forced Maria ... (PAUSE)<br>... to sing with the group. |
| TUTOR: | Three. |
| MAN: | I don't think Peter would have liked ...<br>(PAUSE)<br>... to sing with the group. |
| TUTOR: | Four. |
| MAN: | She couldn't possibly refuse ... (PAUSE)<br>... to sing with the group. |
| TUTOR: | Five. |
| MAN: | She'll never forget ... (PAUSE)<br>... singing with the group. |
| TUTOR: | Six. |
| MAN: | No one made her ... (PAUSE)<br>... sing with the group. |
| TUTOR: | Seven. |
| MAN: | She had never dreamed ... (PAUSE)<br>... of singing with the group. |
| TUTOR: | Eight. |
| MAN: | Peter didn't mind Maria ... (PAUSE)<br>... singing with the group. |
| | |
| TUTOR: | That's the end of exercise A7 – and the end of the ARELS part of Unit 3. |

## UNIT 4    ALTERNATIVES

| | |
|---|---|
| TUTOR: | **Unit 4, Alternatives. Look at page 31, exercise A5.** Here is a talk given by a man from the notes you have. As you listen to his talk, look at the notes and see how he expands them. |
| | |
| MAN: | It's often said that professional sportsmen and women are too well paid. In fact, every time a professional tennis-player, golfer, snooker player or whatever wins thousands of pounds for a tournament, you'll see an article in some newspaper saying how terrible it is.<br><br>But I don't think it's terrible. Professional sportsmen and women are *not* overpaid. After all, they're highly professional people – skilled and talented in their own sports, and most of them have got where they are as the result of years of practice and training. Getting up early every day of the year to go jogging, or training in a gym, or perhaps out on the golf course. A lot of them have had to make personal sacrifices, too. I've heard |

some professional sportsmen and women say that they missed a lot, especially when they were teenagers: while their friends were going out having a good time, they had to go training.

If you take any top athlete, for instance, you'll find he or she spends hours a day practising and keeping fit. And some of the long distance runners run anything up to 100 miles a week in training.

You can't really compare what professional sportsmen and women earn with other people, certainly not with people like shop assistants or bank clerks or dentists. On the other hand, of course, I suppose you could compare them with entertainers, because that's what many of them are. And top entertainers – you know, comedians, singers, film stars and so on – earn a lot of money, so why shouldn't top sportsmen and women?

Oh, I know some of them earn a lot of money teaching and coaching people in their sport, or lecturing, or giving demonstrations or exhibitions. But of course they couldn't do those things, either, without having got to the top of their sport. And many of them won't be at the top of their sport earning thousands for very long. The 'working life' of a professional sportsman can be quite short. Many find they have to retire when they're about 30 – or even before.

So, no, personally I don't think professional sportsmen and women are too well paid.

| | |
|---|---|
| TUTOR: | Now run the cassette back, listen again and do exercise 2. |
| | |
| TUTOR: | **Unit 4. Look at page 31, exercise A7.**<br>Listen to the sentence each time, repeat it and then finish it as you think it should be according to the intonation you hear. We've done the first one for you.<br>One. |
| MAN: | **I don't eat raw vegetables very often myself,**<br>... |
| WOMAN: | **I don't eat raw vegetables very often myself,**<br>but my **parents** do. |
| TUTOR: | Two. |
| MAN: | I don't eat **raw** vegetables very often myself,<br>... (PAUSE) ... but I eat **cooked** ones. |

TUTOR: Three.

WOMAN: I don't **eat** raw vegetables very often myself, ... (PAUSE) ... but I **prepare** them for friends.

TUTOR: Four.

MAN: I don't eat raw vegetables **very** often myself, ... (PAUSE) ... but I eat them **occasionally**.

TUTOR: Five.

WOMAN: I don't eat raw vegetables very often **myself**, ... (PAUSE) ... but most of my **friends** do.

TUTOR: Six.

MAN: I don't eat raw **vegetables** very often myself, ... (PAUSE) ... but I eat raw **meat**.

TUTOR: **Unit 4. Look at page 31, exercise A8.** Listen to the way we make offers and repeat them. Notice the way the speaker's voice rises on the first item and goes down on the second.

MAN: Tea or coffee? (PAUSE)

WOMAN: I can offer you tea or coffee. (PAUSE)

MAN: Would you like tea, or coffee? (PAUSE)

WOMAN: Which would you rather have? Tea or coffee? (PAUSE)

MAN: Do you want to go out or stay in? (PAUSE)

WOMAN: Which would you rather do? Go to the pictures or go bowling? (PAUSE)

TUTOR: That's the end of exercise A8 – and the end of Unit 4.

## UNIT 5   PEOPLE

TUTOR: **Unit 5, People. Look at page 32, exercise A1.** Respond to these five situations, using a two- or three-sentence response wherever possible. The first two items suggest the line you should take. Six.

MAN: You've just discovered that you can't keep a lunch appointment with a colleague tomorrow. You telephone her. Refer to the appointment, explain, apologise, make an excuse and suggest another day. (PAUSE)

TUTOR: Seven.

WOMAN: You have very bad toothache. You phone the dentist's surgery. Explain your problem and ask for an appointment. (PAUSE)

TUTOR: Eight.

MAN: You're sitting with a friend you had a heated argument with a few days ago. You

think it's time to 'clear the air'. What do you say? (PAUSE)

TUTOR: Nine.

WOMAN: You're planning to travel to the capital tomorrow to visit a friend. You've just heard on the radio that there's a one-day public transport strike in the city all day tomorrow. You phone your friend. What do you say? (PAUSE)

TUTOR: Ten.

MAN: You see a young boy sitting crying in the street. You go across to him. What do you say? (PAUSE)

TUTOR: **Unit 5, People. Look at page 33, exercise A2.** An interviewer is talking to Peter Nelson. Peter is a civil engineer. First we'll play the conversation all the way through. Then we'll play it again and ask you some questions. The first time, just listen to get a general idea of what they're saying. Don't worry if you can't understand everything: you should be able to answer the questions even if you miss some of what they're saying. Listen.
Peter has been telling the interviewer about the obligations of a contractor on a civil engineering project such as laying a road or motorway or building a bridge.

*[First playing of the complete interview as below, but with no interruptions]*

TUTOR: Now we're going to play that again, stopping sometimes to ask you a question. You'll know when we're going to ask you a question because you'll hear a noise like this. **PING!** Listen and speak your answers.

INTERVIEWER: And what happens if he does do some work but you find that it's sub-standard in some way?

PETER: Well, it depends how bad it is, but I mean if you don't find it acceptable, then you have to make him do it again.

INTERVIEWER: I bet that doesn't go down well with him. **PING!**

TUTOR: **a)** When might a civil engineer have to make a contractor do a job again? (PAUSE)
**b)** What does 'I bet that doesn't go down well with him' mean? (PAUSE)

INTERVIEWER: ... I bet that doesn't go down well with him.

PETER: Um, no, invariably not.

INTERVIEWER: Have you ever had to make a contractor do something again?

PETER: Yes, I had to make him demolish a bridge he'd once er built.

INTERVIEWER: And how did he react to that?

PETER: Well, he started off by ignoring ah the instruction to remove the bridge, which um was sub-standard in several ways. And nothing happened for quite some time. Er we wrote again repeating the request. **PING!**

TUTOR: **c)** Why did Peter's firm write to the contractor again? (PAUSE)

PETER: ... repeating the request. Er and there was a lot of banter on site about how they'd never get aw- we'd never get away with making them take it down again.

INTERVIEWER: Did you find it difficult as a young engineer, on your first assignment, to actually make a contractor smash down a bridge?

PETER: Well, I went out on(to) site a green engineer effectively. **PING!**

TUTOR: **d)** What does 'green' mean here? (PAUSE)

PETER: ... a green engineer effectively. I made a major contractor break down a bridge which he had just built. The men on site were actually quite pleased because they had been for some time, up until then, quite convinced that their management were er pretty incompetent. And for this to be shown directly was actually a source of er great amusement to them and relief, and they were quite pleased to do the job again properly ... **PING!**

TUTOR: **e)** Why were the men pleased? (PAUSE)

PETER: ... quite pleased to do the job again properly er with the contractor then taking notice of er things like the way the contractor's men do their job. Um, I gained a lot more respect from certainly all the men at site level, if not from the contractor's management.

INTERVIEWER: So the contractor's management and the people who work for them don't always see eye to eye? **PING!**

TUTOR: **f)** What is meant by the expression 'don't always see eye to eye'? (PAUSE)

INTERVIEWER: ... don't always see eye to eye?

PETER: Well, no, um, very often, nowadays especially, um a lot of the work and the

skilled work is sub-contracted to small firms, ... **PING!**

TUTOR: **g)** Does the contractor's firm do all the work? (PAUSE)

PETER: ... is sub-contracted to small firms, perhaps just in the area, who are taken on to do a certain amount of work, and they usually expect to be supported by the main contractor, or the main contractor's labour force, and they aren't always. **PING!**

TUTOR: **h)** 'They aren't always' – what? (PAUSE)

PETER: ... the main contractor's labour force and they aren't always. And if they aren't able to perform, instead of the main contractor asking them why and helping, they very often just withhold payment, and that means that these companies, who may have really stretched themselves to get the work ... **PING!**

TUTOR: **i)** What is meant by 'they may have really stretched themselves'? (PAUSE)

PETER: ... really stretched themselves to get the work because it's the biggest thing that's come to their area, suddenly find that they run out of money and they go to the wall. And that's all to cover the main contractor's inability to manage the job properly. **PING!**

TUTOR: **j)** Why do some small companies 'go to the wall', as Peter puts it? (PAUSE)

TUTOR: **Unit 5. Look at page 33, exercise A3.** Listen to these four people talking and write one, two, three and four in the appropriate boxes, according to the order in which they speak.
One.

WOMAN: I think for us, in the last few years there's been more editorial independence, which of course we appreciate; and we like to think this is reflected in the increased circulation figures. Er, almost the opposite seems to have happened with the tabloids, which some of my colleagues would say is all that the gutter press deserves, but, be that as it may, ... (PAUSE)

TUTOR: Two.

WOMAN: The labour ward, you say? It's up the top of the stairs, past the sign to Casualty on your left, down a little bit of corridor, and just before you get to the X-ray department, it's on your right. OK? (PAUSE)

TUTOR: Three.

MAN: Well, I like to sow in late February, early March, using a lot of good quality peat, and feed 'em regularly through the spring, pinching 'em out near the end of April, er, by which time they're normally an inch, inch and a half, and you'd be surprised, a month or two later you get the most beautiful blooms imaginable. Bulbs? No, I ain't got time for 'em. (PAUSE)

TUTOR: Four.

MAN: Well, yes, your pedals are a bit stiff, but I think I've done something to ease them a bit. But what worries me more is: one or two of the black notes are not really doing their job at all. The B flat above middle C is really shaky. I think a complete overhaul of the keys is going to be necessary soon. (PAUSE)

TUTOR: **Unit 5. Look at page 33, exercsie A4.** Listen to this ansaphone message, which you have to summarise afterwards in thirty seconds.

MARY: I'm afraid John and Mary are not at home at the moment. If you would like to leave a message, please speak after the tone, and one of us will get back to you. *Tone*

BRIAN: Oh, sorry you're not in. I hate these machines. Look, it's all a bit confusing. I wonder if I could ask you to do me a big favour, John. Or Mary. You see, I'm supposed to be meeting the Johnsons' new au pair at the station at six this evening and I know now I just won't be able to make it. I've got tied up seeing some pretty key clients from Edinburgh and there's no chance of it being over before seven at the very earliest. Do you think either you or Mary could get along there to meet her? She's coming on the 4.45 from London, Victoria, which gets in at six minutes past six. I've I've never met her, but I gather she's in her late teens, blonde, with gold-rimmed specs, about average height, and she should be wearing blue. And presumably she'll be carrying a suitcase or two, as she's staying six months with them. Her name's Edith, Edith Schmidt: S.C.H. If you could drive her to the Johnsons' – and that's 44, Greystoke Road, in case you've forgotten – I'd be ever so grateful. They'll be there soon after six thirty, they said. Great, if you could help me out. I'll be in touch. OK? Thanks. 'Bye.

TUTOR: John can't get to the station for six o'clock. He gets in touch with Mary, who's also terribly busy. He passes on the message in as short a time as possible. Listen, then you do the same.

JOHN: Look, Brian says, could you go to the station this evening, pick up the Johnson's new au pair girl and drive her to the Johnsons' house. She's coming on the 4.45 from Victoria, arriving just after six. Her name's Edith Schmidt, she's eighteen, nineteen, blonde, average height, got gold-rimmed glasses, probably wearing blue. And probably with a case or two. The Johnsons will be home soon after 6.30. OK? Oh, the Johnsons' address is 44, Greystoke Road. All right?

TUTOR: That's the end of exercise A4 – and the end of the ARELS part of Unit 5.

## UNIT 6  OUR CHANGING WORLD

TUTOR: **Unit 6, Our Changing World. Look at page 42, exercise A1.** Listen to the way the woman responds in these situations.

MAN: Aren't you tired of learning English?

WOMAN: Far from it. I'm enjoying it now more than ever.

MAN: Could you lend me five pounds until tomorrow?

WOMAN: I'm afraid not. I haven't got a penny on me.

TUTOR: Now respond to these comments in a similar way. One.

MAN: Do you think it's going to rain? (PAUSE)

WOMAN: I wouldn't be surprised. They forecast showers on the radio this morning.

TUTOR: Two.

WOMAN: Where shall we go tonight? (PAUSE)

MAN: It's up to you. I really don't mind, as long we go somewhere.

TUTOR: Three.

MAN: I've got a ten-hour coach journey ahead of me tomorrow. (PAUSE)

WOMAN: Rather you than me. I can't think of anything worse than spending that amount of time on a coach.

TUTOR: Four.

WOMAN: I'm sorry I couldn't make our appointment on Monday. (PAUSE)

MAN: That's quite all right. These things happen.

TUTOR: Five.

MAN: Do you mind if I turn on the TV? (PAUSE)

WOMAN: I'd rather you didn't. I find the television very distracting when I'm working.

TUTOR: **Unit 6. Our Changing World. Look at page 43, exercise A7.** Look at the picture story and listen to someone tell the story of Mr and Mrs Smith, little Johnny and the exploding television. Listen to the way he joins sentences, the way he avoids using the same words all the time, and the way he reports what the characters said.

MAN: The Smith family were watching television one evening last week, Saturday, it must have been, when all of a sudden the screen went blank and a loud bang came from the back of the set. This happened at about a quarter past eight and was most infuriating because it was near the end of the Eurovision Song Contest, which they had been looking forward to seeing for ages. In fact, they had had an early dinner that evening so that they could watch the whole programme together. And then the explosion; end of programme.

Mr Smith, who quite fancies himself as a Do-It-Yourself expert, went off to the garage in search of his tool bag. He was pretty sure that he would be able to put things right quite soon. Meanwhile Johnny was sent protesting upstairs to bed.

Mr Smith set to work, but even after an hour he hadn't made much progress. He had succeeded in unscrewing a number of parts, which were lying all over the place in the sitting room, but his attempts to put them back together again were all in vain. By half past nine he was beginning to get extremely angry.

While his father had been struggling to mend the 'unco-operative' TV, Johnny had been having a bath and getting ready for bed. When he finally came downstairs to say goodnight to his parents, he found his father almost speechless with rage and on the point of giving up.

Johnny asked innocently if he could have a go at repairing the set, saying he had read something about that sort of thing in a comic. But his father was very sceptical: he said it was a job for men, not boys, but eventually agreed to let him have a try. In a matter of minutes, the nine-year-old had fixed the set; in fact the picture was even better than it had been before.

His parents were at a loss to know what to say at first, but a red-faced Mr Smith did in the end allow his son to stay downstairs and watch the Ten O'Clock News with them. At least they were able to find out who had won the Song Contest.

TUTOR: That's the end of exercise A7 – and the end of Unit 6.

## UNIT 7    HOLIDAYS AND TRAVEL

TUTOR: **Unit 7, Holidays and Travel. Look at page 44, exercise A1.** Listen to these sentences. They will each be spoken twice. After each pair, discuss what different 'message' is conveyed each time.

One.

MAN: Would you like something to eat or drink? [*Those are the only two options*]

WOMAN: Would you like something to eat or drink ...? [*Or just sit here / go for a walk?*]

TUTOR: Two.

MAN: We aren't stopping at Birmingham, are we? [*My God! It looks as if we are*]

WOMAN: We aren't stopping at Birmingham, are we? [*I know; I checked the timetable*]

TUTOR: Three.

MAN: Is that the price of a return flight to Paris? [*Or is that for a single?*]

WOMAN: Is that the price of a return flight to Paris? [*Or is that Brussels?*]

TUTOR: Four.

MAN: That was charming, I must say. [*That was extremely rude of him*]

WOMAN: That was charming, I must say. [*That was really lovely*]

TUTOR: Five.

MAN: The reservation is for Mrs J. Smith. [*Not Mr J. Smith!*]

WOMAN: The reservation is for Mrs J. Smith. [*Not Mrs G. Smith!*]

TUTOR: Six.

MAN: The best time to come would be in May or June. [*and only those 2 months*]

WOMAN: The best time to come would be in May or June ... [*or July or maybe August*]

TUTOR: Seven.

MAN: They're arriving on Sunday. [*This is a fact*]

WOMAN: They're arriving on Sunday? [*Why didn't you tell me before?*]

TUTOR: Eight.

MAN: It didn't rain the whole week. [*We had a week of glorious weather!*]

WOMAN: It didn't rain the whole week. [*But very nearly all of it, I can tell you*]

TUTOR: **Unit 7. Look at page 44, exercise A2.**
Listen to the sentences, then practise reading them yourself.
[As in Students' Book]

TUTOR: **Unit 7. Look at page 45, exercise A3.**
Listen to some people starting sentences about their holidays. Decide from their tone of voice whether the statements on page 45 are true or false.
One.

MAN: Well, the food was edible and it didn't rain *every* day, ... [*but ...*]

TUTOR: Two.

WOMAN: Well, the weather was fantastic, the beaches were glorious. [*I loved it*]

TUTOR: Three.

MAN: We thought it would be *easy* to meet the locals ... [*but it wasn't*]

TUTOR: Four

WOMAN: Friends had *warned* us that things were expensive, ... [*but we had no idea they would be that expensive!*]

TUTOR: Five.

MAN: We'd heard that the place was over-commercialised ...[*but it really wasn't*]

TUTOR: Six.

WOMAN: We didn't plan to stay there for a third week ... [*so it's no surprise we didn't*]

TUTOR: **Unit 7. Look at page 45, exercise A5.**
Listen to the dialogue and follow it as you listen. Then read and practise it in pairs.
[Dialogue as in Students' Book.]

TUTOR: That's the end of exercise A5 – and the end of the ARELS part of Unit 7.

## UNIT 8    THIS WORKING LIFE

TUTOR: **Unit 8, This Working Life. Look at page 55 , exercise A2.** Susan, a friend of yours, left a magazine called *Mod Media* at your house or apartment when she dropped in to see you yesterday. She rings and asks you to give her the information contained in an advertisement which she has circled in the 'SITS VACANT' column on page 19 of the magazine. Look at the advertisement on page 54 and take part in the conversation. Ready?

SUSAN: Hello. This is Susan. (PAUSE)
Look, I'm sorry to bother you, but did I leave a copy of last week's 'Mod Media' at your place when I dropped in yesterday? (PAUSE)
So you found it! Thank goodness for that. There was something rather important in it. Do you think you could read it out for me? (PAUSE)
If you look at page 19, you'll find I've circled an ad in the 'Sits Vacant' column. Have you got it? (PAUSE)
Oh, good. Can you tell me exactly what they wanted? Was it a typist, or shorthand typist, or what? (PAUSE)
Oh, yes, I remember. And what sort of experience do they expect? Do people have to have experience in graphics? Or be a first-class typist? What does it say? (PAUSE)
That's fine. What sort of salary are they offering? Was it about £13,000 a year, or was that another job I was looking at? (PAUSE)
Oh, not quite as good as I thought. But perhaps there are some perks. A company car? Luncheon vouchers? Anything like that? (PAUSE)
Well, at least it's got a pension scheme. It sounds good, doesn't it? (PAUSE)
Can you give me the address to write to? (PAUSE)
I've got most of it, but not the street. What was it? Leicester Avenue? How do you spell Leicester? (PAUSE)
Oh, I see. And was there a phone number? (PAUSE)

That's fine. Thanks very much. I think I'll apply. And you can throw the mag away now – unless *you* can find a job in it! Anyway, I'll be in touch again in a few days. 'Bye for now. (PAUSE)

TUTOR: **Unit 8. Look at page 55, exercise A4.** Remember, you work in a small firm and are present at the Annual General Meeting. Listen to some of the things people are saying. You will hear a sentence, and then someone else will start it in a different way. You must finish it so that it means the same thing. Ready?
Seven.

MAN: We'll hear all the reports first, and then we'll discuss them.

WOMAN: We won't ... (PAUSE)

TUTOR: We won't discuss the reports until we've heard them all first.
Eight.

MAN: It's a pity we can't sell more abroad.

WOMAN: What ... (PAUSE)

TUTOR: What a pity we can't sell more abroad.
Nine.

MAN: Someone has suggested we introduce flexi-time.

WOMAN: It's been ... (PAUSE)

TUTOR: It's been suggested that we introduce flexi-time.
Ten.

MAN: We should have introduced profit-sharing last year, then we wouldn't have had all this trouble.

WOMAN: If we ... (PAUSE)

TUTOR: If we had introduced profit-sharing last year, we wouldn't have had all this trouble.
Eleven.

MAN: It'll be necessary for us to advertise abroad this year.

WOMAN: We shall ... (PAUSE)

TUTOR: We shall have to advertise abroad this year.
Twelve.

MAN: We've got too few orders to employ our present workforce.

WOMAN: We haven't ... (PAUSE)

TUTOR: We haven't got enough orders to employ our present workforce.

TUTOR: That's the end of exercise A4 – and the end of Unit 8.

# UNIT 9    SPACESHIP EARTH

TUTOR: **Unit 9, Spaceship Earth. Look at page 56, exercise A1.** Allan Thornton is the Chairman of E.I.A, the Environmental Investigation Agency, which investigates environmental issues worldwide. First we'll play the interview all the way through. Then we'll play part of it again and ask you some questions. The first time, just listen to get a general idea of what Allan's saying. Don't worry if you can't understand everything: you should be able to answer the questions even if you miss some of what they're saying. Listen and do exercise 1.
The aim of the E.I.A. is to discover who is doing environmental damage and how they're doing it, and to obtain actual film and photos of what's going on in order to publicise it.

*[First playing of the complete interview as below, but with no interruptions.]*

TUTOR: Exercise 2. Now we're going to play the last part again, stopping sometimes to ask you a question. You'll know when we're going to ask a question because you'll hear a noise like this. **PING!** Listen and speak your answers.

INTERVIEWER: In 1989, you you had a very, some very successful coverage of a particular issue. Could you ...? I'm talking particularly about the the elephants. How did you set that up?

ALLAN: Well, the elephant um issue is something that we had been researching for about two years. Um two years ago someone came to me that had been involved with a company that was shipping er smuggled er ivory and rhino horn out of East Africa up to the Middle Eastern State of the United Arab Emirates. And this person er gave us some information about the companies involved and the boats they were using, and so on. And we then cross-referenced that with other sources we have, and we found out the companies do exist. We found out that the ships had been in certain ports at certain times, and that really started us on a long trail which led to a two-year investigation of the illegal ivory trade.

We went to the Convention on International Trade in Endangered Species in 1987, and that is an international agreement which is supposed to regulate er the trade in ivory. And when we went to the specific Working Group which was making the regulations for ivory trading, we were surprised to see that there was no voice for conservation of elephants there, and all ... **PING!**

TUTOR: a) What does he mean when he says 'there was no voice for conservation of elephants'? (PAUSE)

ALLAN: ... there was no voice for conservation of elephants there, and all the established groups who people believed were actively working to protect elephants were not there fighting for greater restrictions on the ivory trade. **PING!**

TUTOR: b) Who was working actively to protect elephants from ivory traders? (PAUSE)

ALLAN: ... greater restrictions on the ivory trade. Um what we did find is that the Hong Kong ivory traders and the Japanese ivory traders and the hunters who want to shoot elephants all had their lobbyists there arguing against any more restrictions on ivory trading. **PING!**

TUTOR: c) They all had their lobbyists. What do 'lobbyists' do? (PAUSE)

ALLAN: ... any more restrictions on ivory trading. And we were quite er taken aback by this because er it was certain that the international regulations had massive loopholes, ... **PING!**

TUTOR: d) Why were Allan and his colleagues 'taken aback'? (PAUSE)

ALLAN: ... had massive loopholes, and it was certain that elephants were in very serious decline and that, as far as we could see, the ivory trade needed to be banned totally; ... **PING!**

TUTOR: e) What did they feel should be done, and why? (PAUSE)

ALLAN: ... needed to be banned totally; but here you had the major arguments being made against any further restrictions. And this led to us going further into the issue. So what we did was, we started to track the illegal ivory trade, starting with elephants being killed in Africa, and following the pathways and routes out of Africa, and where the ivory was sent to then into the United Arab Emirates where it was carved and then sent into Hong Kong, ... **PING!**

TUTOR: f) What happened to the ivory in the United Arab Emirates? (PAUSE)

ALLAN: ... and then sent into Hong Kong and Taiwan and Singapore, and those countries then sell it back to the major consuming blocs of Japan, the United States and the European Community. **PING!**

TUTOR: g) What did he mean by 'the major consuming blocs'? (PAUSE)

TUTOR: Exercise 3. You're now going to hear another part of the interview with Allan. Listen carefully and fill in the details about estimated numbers of elephants in the table on page 56.

INTERVIEWER: Allan, you you mentioned the elephant. Could you give us some figures to show the scale of the problem?

ALLAN: OK. The original historical population of elephants in Africa is believed to be about ten million. That was based on the available range and territory that was available for them to occupy. Um in the 1950s it was estimated that there were five million. By 1979 that had declined to 1.5 million. By 1981 it was down to 1.3 million. And the surveys done in 1986 showed that they had declined to around 750,000. The estimated annual kill is something around 100,000 elephants each year. And the present number of elephants left in Africa er is not absolutely clear. It could be anywhere from 300,000 to about 700,000. What we see there is the most rapid and remarkable decline of the biggest land mammal left in the world in the last ten or fifteen years. And if we look forward, we know that African elephants will disappear in East Africa within six years, and within ten years elephants will be virtually wiped out from all of the remaining range er in Africa, unless very urgent measures are taken to protect them.

TUTOR: **Unit 9. Look at page 57, exercise A3.** Now you will hear five more remarks. Respond to them with an appropriate exclamation. Ready? Six.

MAN: And I said to this man: 'Who do you think you are? Some sort of expert on the ecology?' And he said: 'Yes. Actually I'm a lecturer in

environmental studies at the local college.'
(PAUSE)

TUTOR: Seven.

WOMAN: All the trees down the main street in our village have got to come down. They've got something called Dutch Elm disease. (PAUSE)

TUTOR: Eight.

MAN: We weren't expecting it at all, but at last we've got birds nesting in the garden. (PAUSE)

TUTOR: Nine.

WOMAN: The Department of the Environment gives grants to villages that are well kept. We just missed receiving one this year. (PAUSE)

TUTOR: Ten.

MAN: Why should *I* bother about all this pollution business? What can I do about it personally? (PAUSE)

TUTOR: **Unit 9. Look at page 57, exercises A4 and A5**. Now you will hear five more situations in which you might find yourself. Say what it seems natural to say in each situation. Ready? Six.

WOMAN: You meet a neighbour in the street who says: 'It's a gorgeous day, isn't it? We shouldn't complain, I know, but it's all wrong for this time of year.' What do you say? (PAUSE)

TUTOR: Seven.

MAN: You've just finished an important letter and want to catch the post. A friend says she'll be passing a postbox in about five minutes on her way home. What do you say to her? (PAUSE)

TUTOR: Eight.

WOMAN: A mechanic friend of yours has tuned your car engine so that it will run on unleaded petrol, but he won't take any payment for it. What do you say to him? (PAUSE)

TUTOR: Nine.

MAN: Yesterday you promised to buy an 'ozone friendly' air freshener for a friend from a shop you know, but you forgot. What do you say when she asks you where it is and how much she owes you for it? (PAUSE)

TUTOR: Ten.

WOMAN: Some people you know have a small clump of trees in their garden and are thinking of cutting them all down to make a vegetable patch to grow their own vegetables. They ask you what you think of the idea. What do you say? (PAUSE)

TUTOR: That's the end of exercise A5 – and the end of the ARELS part of Unit 9.

## UNIT 10  YOU AND YOUR FOOD

TUTOR: **Unit 10, You and Your Food. Look at page 66, exercise A2**. You're working in a takeaway restaurant taking orders. A woman rings in to order some food. Look at the menu and take part in the conversation. Ready?

WOMAN: Hello. Is that the Choosy Takeaway? (PAUSE)
I'd like to order some food. First of all, what starters have you got? (PAUSE)
Sorry. What were the two kinds of soup again? (PAUSE)
And how much are the different starters? (PAUSE)
Oh, fine. And what about main dishes? What sorts of pies do you do, for instance? (PAUSE)
That's a good choice. How much are they? (PAUSE)
And what do you serve with them? Chips? Or jacket potato? Or rice perhaps? (PAUSE)
Oh, that's good. And what vegetables have you got? (PAUSE)
That's marvellous. And I suppose you'll tell me you do side salads as well. (PAUSE)
It's amazing. Most take-aways only do one sort of food. – Well, before I order, just one last thing. Do you do any sweets? (PAUSE)
Home-made ice cream. Lovely. Well, I'd like to order now. The first thing I want is one prawn cocktail and one tomato soup ...

TUTOR: **Unit 10. Look at page 67, exercise A3**. Listen carefully to the sentences and repeat them.
[As in Students' Book.]

TUTOR: **Unit 10. Look at page 67, exercise A4** and listen to the conversation.
[As in Students' Book.]

TUTOR: That's the end of exercise A4 – and the end of Unit 10.

## UNIT 11   WEIRD AND WONDERFUL

TUTOR: **Unit 11, Weird and Wonderful. Look at page 68, exercise A3,** and the picture story on page 69. Listen to someone telling the story and notice the language she uses.

WOMAN: A couple of years ago Tony and Carol had a very strange experience. They'd been looking forward to their holiday for a long time. They had been saving for nearly a year and now they were off for a fortnight in the mountains. Soon after they set off, they saw a hitchhiker by the side of the road, and, perhaps because they were in such a good mood, they stopped to offer him a lift. He was a pleasant-looking man, probably in his early forties; he was wearing a suit and had no luggage. They thought it was strange to see him there on a country road in the middle of nowhere, but they didn't try to find out what he was doing there. He asked them if they could take him to the nearest station, about twenty kilometres away. After they'd driven about ten kilometres, they came to a café by the side of the road. The man, who had introduced himself as Harry Watt, suggested they should stop, so that he could buy them a drink as a way of thanking them for the lift. While they were sitting in the café, Tony and Carol showed him on their map where they intended to go during their two weeks in the mountains. When they had finished their coffees, they went outside again and Tony was just about to go round to the driver's door of the car when the stranger pulled him back. Tony hadn't noticed that an enormous lorry was speeding past just at that moment and would probably have killed him if he'd taken another step forward. Tony couldn't thank the man enough and joked about how glad he was that they'd decided to stop in the first place. A little while later they arrived at the station and they said goodbye to their passenger. That evening, after dinner in their hotel, Tony opened the local paper and was amazed to see a headline and a photograph that completely took his breath away. The photograph was of the hitchhiker they had met that morning and the headline read: 'Death of Famous Tycoon'. The article went on to say that the man they had picked up had died two days previously. That day was a day they will never forget.

TUTOR: **Unit 11. Look at page 68, exercise A4.**
Say that Carol is – or was – the same as Tony in these situations. Use 'So ...' or 'Nor ...' Ready?
One.
MAN: Tony'll never forget that day. (PAUSE)
WOMAN: Nor will Carol.
TUTOR: Two.
MAN: At first Tony was surprised to see the man. (PAUSE)
WOMAN: So was Carol.
TUTOR: Three.
MAN: Tony'd never seen the man before. (PAUSE)
WOMAN: Nor had Carol.
TUTOR: Four.
MAN: Tony couldn't believe it when he read the newspaper. (PAUSE)
WOMAN: Nor could Carol.
TUTOR: Five.
MAN: Tony wouldn't have let him into his car if he'd known who he was. (PAUSE)
WOMAN: Nor would Carol.
TUTOR: Six.
MAN: Tony had never believed in ghosts until then. (PAUSE)
WOMAN: Nor had Carol.
TUTOR: Seven.
MAN: Tony's really a very level-headed sort of person. (PAUSE)
WOMAN: So is Carol.
TUTOR: Eight.
MAN: Tony still has nightmares about that day. (PAUSE)
WOMAN: So does Carol.

TUTOR: **Unit 11. Look at page 68, exercise A5.**
Agree with this man using short tags.
Here are two more examples:
MAN: It was a frightening experience.
WOMAN: Yes, it was, wasn't it?
MAN: It can't have been very pleasant.
WOMAN: No, it can't, can it?

TUTOR: Now you do it.
One.

MAN: It's amazing that things like that happen. (PAUSE)

WOMAN: Yes, it is, isn't it?

TUTOR: Two.

MAN: You quite often hear of stories like that, though. (PAUSE)

WOMAN: Yes, you do, don't you?

TUTOR: Three.

MAN: As far as I remember, the man looked very normal. (PAUSE)

WOMAN: Yes, he did, didn't he?

TUTOR: Four.

MAN: But his eyes weren't normal. (PAUSE)

WOMAN: No, they weren't, were they?

TUTOR: Five.

MAN: They had no colour. (PAUSE)

WOMAN: No, they didn't, did they?

TUTOR: Six.

MAN: It'd be terrible to be in a situation like that. (PAUSE)

WOMAN: Yes, it would, wouldn't it?

TUTOR: **Unit 11. Look at page 68, exercise A6.**
Reword these sentences beginning with the word or words you hear after each sentence. Here are two examples.

MAN: The couple were very frightened by the experience.

TUTOR: The couple found ...

WOMAN: The couple found the experience very frightening.

WOMAN: They had never seen the man before.

TUTOR: It was ...

MAN: It was the first time they had ever seen the man.

TUTOR: Now you do it.
One.

MAN: They saw the man while they were driving towards the mountains.

TUTOR: They were ... (PAUSE)

WOMAN: They were driving towards the mountains when they saw the man.

TUTOR: Two.

MAN: "Where are you going?" the man said to them.

TUTOR: The man asked them ... (PAUSE)

WOMAN: The man asked them where they were going.

TUTOR: Three.

MAN: They said they would give the man a lift to the nearest station.

TUTOR: They offered ... (PAUSE)

WOMAN: They offered to give the man a lift to the nearest station.

TUTOR: Four.

MAN: "Very kind of you both to give me a lift," said the man.

TUTOR: The man thanked ... (PAUSE)

WOMAN: The man thanked them both for giving him a lift.

TUTOR: Five.

MAN: They didn't think it was strange until they saw the newspaper.

TUTOR: It was only ... (PAUSE)

WOMAN: It was only when they saw the newspaper that they thought it was strange.

TUTOR: Six.

MAN: This all happened because they stopped to give the man a lift.

TUTOR: None of this ... (PAUSE)

WOMAN: None of this would have happened if they hadn't stopped to give the man a lift.

TUTOR: **Unit 11. Look at page 69, exercise A7.**
Listen to these examples.

TUTOR: Example one.
It was strange, wasn't it?

WOMAN: 'Strange'?! It was really weird!

TUTOR: Example two.
It was quite a nice day.

MAN: 'Quite nice'?! It was a glorious day!

TUTOR: Now you do it. Disagree with the following statements in the same way. There are no 'correct' responses, but we've suggested some. Ready? One.

MAN: The man was quite well dressed. (PAUSE)

WOMAN: 'Quite well dressed'?! He was extremely smart!

TUTOR: Two.

WOMAN: They were surprised when they saw the man's photo in the paper. (PAUSE)

MAN: 'Surprised'?! They must have been absolutely amazed.

TUTOR: Three.

MAN: Perhaps it was a bit silly to stop for the man. (PAUSE)

WOMAN: 'Silly'? It was an idiotic thing to do.

TUTOR: Four.

WOMAN: The man talked about himself for quite a

MAN: long time, didn't he? (PAUSE)

MAN: 'Quite a long time'? He talked about himself for ages and ages!

TUTOR: Five.

MAN: I seem to remember it was quite hot that day. (PAUSE)

WOMAN: 'Quite hot'? It was absolutely boiling!

TUTOR: Six.

WOMAN: It's a difficult story to believe, isn't it? (PAUSE)

MAN: 'Difficult'? It's absolutely incredible!

TUTOR: That's the end of exercise A7 – and the end of the ARELS part of Unit 11.

## UNIT 12   PROBLEMS AND SOLUTIONS

TUTOR: **Unit 12, Problems and Solutions. Look at page 78, A1**. Listen to the passage and follow it in your book.
[As in Students' Book.]

TUTOR: **Unit 12. Look at page 78, exercise A2**. Chris Windley talks to our interviewer about an 'escape and evade' exercise he had to take part in when he was a young trainee naval officer some years ago. The exercise took place in Galloway in the west of Scotland. First we'll play the interview all the way through. Then we'll play it again and ask you some questions. The first time, just listen to get a general idea of what Chris is saying. Don't worry if you can't understand everything: you should be able to answer the questions even if you miss some of what they're saying. Listen and do exercise 1. *[First playing of the complete interview as below, but with no interruptions.]*

TUTOR: Now we're going to play that again, stopping sometimes to ask you a question. You'll know when we're going to ask a question because you'll hear a noise like this. **PING!** Listen and speak your answers.

CHRIS: Now ultimately what happened to us was that we er decided that ... that there was an area, a territory in which we were allowed to er ... this exercise could take place in, and we decided that it it wasn't relevant any

more, that the exercise area didn't exist for the purposes of this, and that if it was going to be this serious, we would ... why should we stay within the bounds of the exercise area? So we walked out of outside the exercise area and up to our objective and actually got behind our objective er and then and then waited for er- everybody to arrive. **PING!**

TUTOR: **a)** From what you've heard, what do you think the objective of the exercise was? (PAUSE)

CHRIS: ... er- everybody to arrive. So at the time this was er looked ... was frowned upon quite considerably by some people, you know. **PING!**

TUTOR: **b)** What does 'frowned upon' mean here? (PAUSE)

CHRIS: ... was frowned upon quite considerably by some people, you know. It's cheating in a way.

INTERVIEWER: Yeh, cheating, yes.

CHRIS: Well, some people would call it cheating, but what what's cheating and what's initiative? **PING!**

TUTOR: **c)** What did they do that was perhaps cheating or using their initiative? (PAUSE)

CHRIS: ... but what what's cheating and what's initiative?

INTERVIEWER: Quite, yes. So you were out in the open for six days then (Hm.), um, and you weren't given any food or shelter?

CHRIS: We had some rations. We did have some rations. We had no shelter other than what you call um erm capes, bivouac capes, which would, could turn into small tents. **PING!**

TUTOR: **d)** How was the interviewer's assumption wrong? (PAUSE)

CHRIS: ... which would, could turn into small tents. So those w- those were what we sheltered in and other than that, you know, we could ... again, you always had this dilemma of, I mean, there were huts and houses, you know, there, but these were sort of not allowed to be used. But again, you know, you would er say to yourself: well, again, is is this relevant, you know? **PING!**

TUTOR: **e)** What do you think Chris's dilemma was? (PAUSE)

CHRIS: ... well, again, is is this relevant, you know? Why can't I just go and break into one of these? I think we actually did break into one. **PING!**

TUTOR: **f)** What did they break into? (PAUSE)

CHRIS: ... I think we actually did break into one.

INTERVIEWER: For shelter?

CHRIS: Yeh, we did, yes. Well, that that happened because one of our guys er was erm, well, we considered him to be suffering from hyperthermia; and er so w- what we said was: you know, well, this guy could die here. **PING!**

TUTOR: **g)** Why were they so worried about the man? (PAUSE)

CHRIS: ... you know, well, this guy could die here. And erm I think that we we broke into a hut. And we also smashed up a boat to use for firewood to keep this this this chap warm. **PING!**

TUTOR: **h)** What was the firewood for? (PAUSE)

CHRIS: ... to use for firewood to keep this this this chap warm. You know er again it's very difficult, you see, to s to simulate survival conditions. 'Cos this guy could have died and we weren't going to let him die. So we smashed the boat up. And made firewood out of it. **PING!**

TUTOR: **i)** What do you think the weather was like during the exercise? (PAUSE)

CHRIS: ... So we smashed the boat up. And made firewood out of it.

INTERVIEWER: Did the people who organised this exercise consider you to have done well in the end?

CHRIS: Well, it never affected our promotion. **PING!**

TUTOR: **j)** Do you have the impression that Chris was promoted later in his navy career? (PAUSE)

TUTOR: **Unit 12. Look at page 79, exercise A3.** Complete the unfinished sentences so that they mean the same as the one before it each time. They all have something to do with problems of various kinds. Listen first to these two examples:

WOMAN: There are a lot of road accidents because people don't think enough when they're driving.

TUTOR: If people ...

MAN: If people thought more when they were driving, there wouldn't be so many road accidents.

WOMAN: Unemployment causes a lot of domestic problems.

TUTOR: A lot of ...

MAN: A lot of domestic problems are caused by unemployment.

TUTOR: Now you do it. Six.

WOMAN: It might seem strange, but we just haven't got enough information.

TUTOR: Strange ... (PAUSE)

MAN: Strange as it might seem, we just haven't got enough information.

TUTOR: Seven.

WOMAN: You'll have to cut out bread and potatoes if you want to lose weight.

TUTOR: The only way ... (PAUSE)

MAN: The only way you'll lose weight is by cutting out bread and potatoes.

TUTOR: Eight.

WOMAN: This piano ought to be tuned immediately.

TUTOR: This piano needs ... (PAUSE)

MAN: This piano needs tuning immediately.

TUTOR: Nine.

WOMAN: Getting rid of that hedge would give us more space in the garden.

TUTOR: If we ... (PAUSE)

MAN: If we got rid of that hedge, we would have more space in the garden.

TUTOR: Ten.

WOMAN: If you have any more problems, just come and see me.

TUTOR: Should ... (PAUSE)

MAN: Should you have any more problems, just come and see me.

TUTOR: That's the end of exercise A3 – and the end of Unit 12.